MEDIEVALISM
A MANIFESTO

PAST IMPERFECT

Past Imperfect presents concise critical overviews of the latest research by the world's leading scholars. Subjects cross the full range of fields in the period ca. 400—1500 CE which, in a European context, is known as the Middle Ages. Anyone interested in this period will be enthralled and enlightened by these overviews, written in provocative but accessible language. These affordable paperbacks prove that the era still retains a powerful resonance and impact throughout the world today.

Director and Editor-in-Chief

Simon Forde, *Western Michigan University*

Acquisitions Editor

Ruth Kennedy, *Adelaide*

Production

Linda K. Judy, *Kalamazoo*

MEDIEVALISM
A MANIFESTO

Richard Utz

Library of Congress Cataloging in Publication Data

A catalogue record for this book is available from the Library of Congress.

© 2017, Arc Humanities Press, Kalamazoo and Bradford

ISBN 978-1-942401-02-5
e-ISBN 978-1-942401-03-2

mip-archumanitiespress.org

Printed and bound by CPI Group (UK) Ltd, Croydon, CR0 4YY

Contents

List of Illustrations

Foreword

This book* is called a *manifesto* because it has an unapologetically political objective. I want to help reform the way we think about and practise our academic engagement with medieval culture, and I will use my observations as a medievalist and medievalism-ist over the last twenty-five years to offer ways in which we might reconnect with the general public that has allowed us to become, since the late nineteenth century, a rather exclusive clan of specialists communicating mostly with each other.

Many considerations have played a role in my decision to address this subject: most importantly, my experience of going back and forth across the Atlantic and living, teaching, and writing within different cultural and educational contexts for the study of the Middle Ages. As a result, much of my scholarship shows traces of an identity anchored both in places, traditions, and rituals dating back to medieval culture and also in manifestations spatially, temporally, and politically removed from medieval culture. In addition, I believe my ideas relate to a larger set of questions currently asked by students, parents, journalists, politicians, and academic advisory boards about the relevance and value of the humanities and social sciences in radically new contexts for knowledge production and reception.

I wanted to write a volume for Past Imperfect because this new series allows for a concise monograph written in a somewhat "edgy" style. In my last monograph, *Chaucer and the Discourse of German Philology* (2002), I managed to include as many paratextual features (footnotes, annotated bibliography, general bibliography, and so on) as actual scholarly narrative. It was the fruit of nine years of reading and research, and its audience, while appreciative, was rather small and comprised a few handfuls of colleagues worldwide also working in the reception history of Geoffrey Chaucer. Like *Chaucer and the Discourse of German Philology*, this new monograph also wants to speak to my colleagues, but to many more of them, and it wants to entice them to look beyond our traditional academic audiences in a variety of ways. I am grateful to Simon Forde and Ruth Kennedy, for launching Past Imperfect and for curating my volume into shape. The series itself is an excellent example of the kind of medievalism I propose.

Like every member of the academy, I could list a whole host of teachers, colleagues, and friends who have played a role in shaping my views on engaging with the Middle Ages. Among them, however, Kathleen Verduin (Hope College) and the late Leslie J. Workman (1927–2001) stand out as the two without whose personal and professional support I would not have been able to bridge my own pastist German philological roots with more presentist and often continuist Anglo-American academic approaches. Together with them, and the members of the international and interdisciplinary community of scholars they brought together in the International Society for the Study of Medievalism, I was not only able to historicize the *longue durée* of the postmedieval reception of the Middle Ages, but also to situate my own place within this process.

* Portions of chapters 1 and 2 were presented as the plenary at the 50th International Congress on Medieval Studies at Western Michigan University in 2015 (later in part condensed into "Don't Be Snobs, Medievalists" for the *Chronicle of Higher Education*, April 4, 2016). Some shorter sections in chapter 1 were previously published as "'Mes souvenirs sont peut-être reconstruits': Medieval Studies, Medievalism, and the Scholarly and Popular Memories of the 'Right of the Lord's First Night,'" *Philologie im Netz* 31 (2005); sections of chapter 3 were previously presented at the 30th International Annual Conference on Medievalism (Washington & Jefferson College, 2015) and the 51st International Congress on Medieval Studies (2016); and sections of chapter 4 were previously presented at the 48th International Congress on Medieval Studies (2013). Finally, an earlier version of chapter 5, "Medievalism and the Subject of Religion," was published in *Studies in Medievalism* 25 (2015). I would like to acknowledge all who commented on and enriched my conference papers, and I thank the editors and publishers for their permission to include previously published materials.

Chapter 1

What's Love Got to Do with It?
Our Middle Ages, Ourselves

> *I've been taking on a new direction*
> *But I have to say*
> *I've been thinking about my own protection*
> *It scares me to feel this way [...]*
> Tina Turner (1984)

The photograph on the cover of this scholarly *essai* was taken in 1954. As you can see, the couple are dressed in premodern garb, handmade to resemble the clothes worn by nobles and well-to-do citizens in the Bavarian city of Amberg on the occasion of the lavish wedding festivities for Margarete, daughter of Duke Ludwig IX of Bavaria, with Philip the Upright, Elector Palatine of the Rhine, in 1474. A historical pageant of the wedding was written in 1934 as part of the celebrations, spearheaded by Josef Filbig, the Nazi mayor of Amberg, on the 900th anniversary of the first recorded mention of the city. The 1954 performance featured an apparently revised version of the original 1934 pageant, and once again Josef Filbig was mayor of Amberg, this time democratically elected with 64 per cent of the vote as candidate for the right-wing party *Deutsche Gemeinschaft*. The man in the picture, a music teacher, served as the choir director for the performance. More on this in chapter 3.

One year before the picture was taken, the woman and the man had married in the Baroque Mariahilf Pilgrimage church, built during the Thirty Years' War because Christians in the region believed the Virgin Mary had saved their city from one of the many occurrences of the plague. The couple, like most Amberg Catholics, participated in the annual pilgrimage to the miraculous image of the Madonna, created as a copy of painter Lukas Cranach's 1537 image of the Virgin in Innsbruck Cathedral.

When the man in the picture was seventeen, the woman was eleven, brownshirts with pickaxes entered the city's synagogue and set fire to the furniture and ritual objects. Authorities would justify these actions as well as the subsequent deportation of many of the city's Jews by retelling stories of alleged Jewish ritual murder, host desecration, and usury, all three constitutive elements of the medieval Christian identity virulent until and even beyond the Second Vatican Council in 1962–65.

The woman in the picture would come to teach at two Catholic middle schools run by the School Sisters of Notre Dame, a nineteenth-century order founded to counteract secular modern education. The man in the picture would, after a career in teaching and school administration, be dubbed a knight of the Equestrian Order of the Holy Sepulchre, a Catholic chivalric order that traces its origins back to Godfrey of Bouillon, the leader of the First Crusade, and whose mission is to reinforce the practice of Christian life and to sustain and assist the religious, spiritual, charitable, and social works of the Catholic Church in the Holy Land.

The couple would have two sons, whom they raised in the Catholic faith tradition and who grew up in a media culture steeped in Anglo-American representations of medieval chivalry or their cultural descendants from King Arthur, Ivanhoe, and Robin Hood through Prince Valiant and Zorro. One of their sons would later become a medievalist, write his doctoral dissertation on Geoffrey Chaucer, investigate the unsettling longevity of the medieval ritual murder accusation against Jews, advocate for the critical examination of religion as a major factor in the permanence of medieval imagery and cultural practices through contemporaneity, and expose some of the continuities between Third Reich and post-Third Reich medieval scholarship and revivalist popular festivals in Germany. He also wrote an essay on a French 1960s TV series, *Thierry la Fronde*, which "Frenched" the story of Robin Hood. His wife, a Frenchwoman, introduced him to that TV series. It was special to her because she had had her first crush at the age of three on the Belgian lead actor, Jean-Claude Drouot. The medievalist son later moved from Germany to the US. There he wrote a book on the reception of Chaucer in the German-speaking world, including a chapter on a nineteenth-century German predecessor philologist, Ewald Flügel, who also moved from the University of Leipzig to Stanford University.

Lest you are already bored by this thinly veiled academic "selfie," I will stop this narrative and reveal that the woman and the man in the picture are my parents, Hildegard (1927–) and Clement Utz (1921–2005). What the collation of some seminal stations in my biography with several of my published academic titles is supposed to suggest is that my (and many others') admission ticket to studying and teaching medieval culture has been deeply affective and personal; and that the more open negotiation of these affective and personal motivations to learning about medievalia is perhaps the most important difference between the prevailing notion of the

Middle Ages roughly fifty years ago and our contemporary notion. Thus, I will claim that while as medievalists we have become more inclusive geographically (the Mediterranean), culturally (Muslim medievalisms), methodologically (digital media), and linguistically (minority languages), and while we have greater access to more edited medieval texts as well as manuscripts, and have generally amassed more detailed knowledge about more aspects of medieval culture than ever before, our most decisive step forward, I feel, has not been quantitative, but qualitative. Let me mention some examples of this process.

In the spring of 2003, Jacques Le Goff, one of the international figureheads of medieval studies in the second half of the twentieth century, published *À la recherche du Moyen-Âge*. This was both a biographical account of how he became a medievalist and a manifesto for the kind of history practised by the École des Annales. Based on a series of interviews, Le Goff's memoir was written for an audience consisting of medieval scholars as well as an educated general reading public, as it still exists in contemporary France; that section of "Old Europe," mind you, where intellectuals, even medievalists, unabashedly play an essential role in public life.

While Le Goff cannot for the world remember why, at the age of ten, he decided he would want to study history, he does recall that it was Walter Scott's historical novel, *Ivanhoe* (1819) that excited him about the Middle Ages. Scott's narrative used, according to Le Goff, certain material traits of the Middle Ages—the forest between Sheffield and Doncaster, the siege of Torquilstone castle, the tournament at Ashby with its audience of peasants, merchants, courtly ladies, knights, monks, and priests—to create an impression of verisimilitude that captured Le Goff's imagination and set him on the track towards becoming a medievalist.

Le Goff adds the disclaimer that he did not really decide at this tender age that he would centre his later efforts on the material aspects of medieval culture. However, long is the list of realistic attractions in *Ivanhoe* to which he would later dedicate scholarly articles and books. In fact, if we may place any trust in Le Goff's recollections, his youthful reading experience would well up at ever so many decisive junctures of his biography. Sometimes the connections with the first medievalist novel he read were little more than vague analogues, as when the audiences at soccer and rugby matches remind him of the audiences at Ashby (18). At other times, however, such remembrances of childhood reading were quite specific, as when the tribulations and trials of the beautiful Rebecca of York, who is accused of witchcraft, sway the adolescent Le Goff to enlist in a political organization, the Front Populaire, which opposed the growing anti-Semitism and racism in pre-occupation France (12).

Further analysis of Le Goff's book exhibits a remarkable dichotomy. While he attempts to establish an affective basis for his choice of becoming a medievalist by tracing medieval memories back to his first encounters with Walter Scott, connect his interest in twentieth-century politics with his reactions to episodes in *Ivanhoe*, and stress the advent of cinematic representations of the past (including Richard Thorpe's 1952 film version; 12, 19), he quickly diminishes such memories as nostalgic and draws clear boundaries between scientific and serious research in medieval culture on the one hand and indistinct images or ideas about the Middle Ages as represented in popular culture or the historical novel on the other. In a section during which he explains how, as an adolescent, he found the same degrees of fascinating alterity in twentieth-century Roman Catholic liturgical ritual and, once again, that omnipresent tournament at Ashby, he cautions his readers by intimating that "perhaps my memories are reconstructed" (20). He feels he cannot trust his own recollections, assuming perhaps that the truth value of any memoir will necessarily suffer from a personal post-hoc perspective, an attitude that would fabricate a linear teleology for a scholar who moved in one *grand récit* from reading *Ivanhoe* to teaching at the Sorbonne.

Le Goff's demarcation between subjective memoir and scholarly investigation is, in fact, a topos among medievalists whose dominant discursive standards demand that the investigating subject's affective connection be kept from colouring the subjects of investigation. Nothing better exemplifies this topos than the introductory section in Horst Fuhrmann's 1997 *Einladung ins Mittelalter* in which he wishes that his book, intended as an "invitation" to medieval culture for a general audience, would close shut automatically if any professional historian tried to open and read it. Fuhrmann then confesses: "I hope it will be neither to the disadvantage of the subject matter nor the author if he admits that he had fun to explain himself to a readership of non-specialists: to sketch his own Middle Ages" (10). Revealingly, by moving from the first person to the third person in the same sentence, Fuhrmann performs grammatically most twentieth-century academic medievalists' agonistic subject position towards pre- and extra-academic interest in medieval culture.

Kathleen Biddick has identified the historical period, methods, and motivations that led to the demarcation between academic and extra-academic interest in the Middle Ages. In her 1998 book, the *Shock of Medievalism*, she writes:

In order to separate and elevate themselves from popular studies of medieval culture, the new academic medievalists of the nineteenth century designated their practices, influenced by positivism, as scientific and eschewed what they regarded as less-positivist, "nonscientific" practices, labeling them medievalism. [...]

Gaston Paris's insistence on documentary readings of medieval poetry in his new philology severed the study of medieval literature from poetics. Viollet-le-Duc produced a scientific medieval art history by splitting off images from their material milieu. [Bishop] Stubbs refused to teach any constitutional history beyond the seventeenth century on the grounds that it was too presentist. Through these different kinds of exclusions, justified as avoiding sentimental medievalisms, these scholars were able to imagine a coherent inside to the discipline of medieval studies. Medievalism, a fabricated effect of this newly forming medieval studies, thus became visible as its despised "other," its exteriority. (2)

Biddick goes on to illustrate how recent critical histories of this moment of rupture, while rejecting the "fathers" of medieval studies and exposing their often nationalist and imperialist objectives, never sufficiently challenged the scientific and science-like techniques and conventional pastist chronology of medieval studies. Rather, while exponentially increasing our knowledge about the lively history of the discipline, they stopped short of the kind of engagement with the medieval past that would imagine, in Biddick's words, "temporality as something other than hard-edged alterity" (10).

Kathleen Biddick, Aranye Fradenburg, and Carolyn Dinshaw, to name only a few, have championed such atemporal approaches; and I view Dinshaw's 2012 book, *How Soon is Now: Medieval Texts, Amateur Readers, and the Queerness of Time*, as a signpost as well as a catalyst for what a creative merging of so-called amateurish and academic approaches to the Middle Ages might yield. Those of us convinced that the future of medieval studies can only be ensured by forming the tortoise and communicating only amongst each other will find *How Soon Is Now* a difficult read, as Dinshaw idealizes the figure of the amateur, whom university-educated full-time professors have scapegoated as their eternal "other" since the late nineteenth century. Into her narrative of how to arrive at her own ideal moment of "Now," this "moment that is not detached and not disenchanted" in "a more just and more attached nonmodernity" (39), Dinshaw weaves various moments, from undergraduate student through accomplished scholar, when she herself was and felt like an amateur, when she negotiated what Jesse Swan once aptly called "the one quality forbidden the late modern professor": Love.[1] Dinshaw celebrates what she calls her own "queer kinship" with the "amateur's" kind of "love," that most basic "delight" felt by those whom we brand as "dilettantes," that presentist or *everyday*-ist pleasure felt by the unhistorical "*jour*nalist," the desire felt by the mere "enthusiast" Plato warned us about, who is possessed by and obsessed with answering questions about the past in one's own present as well as in ever so many moments of receptions of medieval culture throughout and across the *longe durée* that is the postmedieval.

Foregrounding and conjoining each of her book chapters with what she terms her own "uncertain progress and uneven development as a medievalist and queer" (32–33), Dinshaw tells us about a whole host of predecessor colleagues whose degree of intimacy with their subject matter and materials queered their relation with linear temporality. There is enthusiast-editor-polymath Frederick James Furnivall, who teamed up with philologists only to make sure that large English audiences would enjoy and learn from medieval texts; poet-scholar Henry Wadsworth Longfellow, who was fascinated with the *Golden Legend*; fairy tale collector-editor Andrew Lang, who wrote a comic letter to Sir John Mandeville; Eton provost and author of a Mandeville parody, M. R. James; author Washington Irving and his fictional alter ego, "Geoffrey Crayon", who admired King James's *Kingis Quair*; editor-amateur Hope Emily Allen, who rendered *The Book of Margery Kempe* accessible to twentieth-century readers; and film character Thomas Colpeper from the little known 1944 movie *A Canterbury Tale*, a patriotic amateur historian, magistrate, and criminal who strains to connect an indifferent audience of soldiers and local women with Chaucer's poetry.

Dinshaw's book, with its effective rhetorical, structural, and methodological integration of the personal and the professional, the confessional and the critical, and the self-reflexive and the "seriously" academic, demonstrates that scholarship is always deeply autobiographical. When Leslie J. Workman, the founder of Anglo-American medievalism studies, tried to build a space for studying the reception of the Middle Ages after the Middle Ages in the 1980s and 1990s based on his own personal exposure to the unique continuity that characterizes the Anglo-American tradition, he ran into everything from indifference to downright disdain among medievalists and publishers, most of whom dismissed him as an amateur because he did not have a doctoral degree and had lost his academic appointment when his college closed. However, even an eminent tenured medievalist like Norman Cantor would find himself at the receiving end of his academic colleagues' scorn because, as the *New York Times* obituary stated, he had a "graceful prose style and [...] narrative drive that made his books unusually readable."[2] When, like Workman, he confirmed with his 1991 book, *Inventing the Middle Ages* that all scholarship was autobiography and that the multitude of scholarly endeavours to recuperate the Middle Ages had only resulted in ever so many (subjective) reinventions of that period, many reviewers treated him as if he had fouled the field and its founding fathers, from Marc Bloch, Ernst Robert Curtius, Étienne Gilson, Charles Homer Haskins, Johan Huizinga, Ernst Kantorowicz, David Knowles, C. S. Lewis, Erwin Panofsky, Percy Ernst Schramm, J. R. Strayer, and J. R. R. Tolkien, Cantor had to write an extra book, the fully-fledged and tongue-in-cheek autobiography, *Inventing Norman Cantor* (2002), in which he reaffirmed that the "ultimate task and obligation of a historian" was to make history "communicable to and accessible by the educated public at large" (223), and that it is "the happiness and sadness of our own lives" (228) that shapes our academic research and scholarship. In a letter to Workman, Cantor summed up what he saw as the main challenge for anyone attempting to lower the drawbridge towards a larger reading public for medievalia:

> The fact of the matter is that most professional medievalists are not going to support actively what you are doing—it is too activist, for one thing. Secondly, the more "medievalism" is studied the more their own work will be judged from that perspective and they fear it will be found wanting, as it will. [...] The fact is that there is still a well of inspiration out there in the general culture. My book has tapped into it, while sneaking under the wire, more or less, of academic respectability. Whether you and your wife [Kathleen Verduin] realize it or not, you are doing something more bold; you are challenging the bastion of medievalist academia by conjuring up a general cultural movement. All power to you.[3]

What differentiates Dinshaw's book from the efforts by most colleagues who practise what we call, with varying success, "medievalism" is that her cutting the cord of linear temporality and integrating her affective relationship to the Middle Ages protect her from having to swear allegiance to medieval studies or medievalism.

In a 2010 essay, "Chaucer's American Accent," David Matthews situated the semantic and methodological quagmire surrounding both terms and practices:

> There is a strong suggestion [...] that what tends to happen over time is that medieval studies passes into medievalism; as it ceaselessly updates itself, medieval studies expels what it no longer wishes to recognize as part of itself. Among late-twentieth-century works, we could consider the example of D. W. Robertson's *A Preface to Chaucer* (1962) and ask whether it is going the same way. In contemporary Chaucer criticism, Robertson's work is chiefly cited to point out where it went wrong, to highlight the follies of exegetical criticism. In other words, its function has become one of differentiation—modern scholarship marks itself out by comparison with it, just as literary and political histories previously marked themselves out against [Thomas] Warton and [Bishop] Stubbs. Such works are expelled from medieval studies and become medievalism. [...] This is a process which continues so that medievalism studies risks being no more than a sifting through the *disjecta membra* of medieval studies.[4]

Matthews's reminder of the shifting fate of D. W. Robertson's paradigm of patristic exegesis, which was one of the constitutive practices comprising the notion of the Middle Ages from the 1950s through the 1970s, contains clear manifestations of time, movement, and process, three areas that conceptual historians have established as one of the central tenets of modern thought. In *Futures Past: On the Semantics of Historical Time* (2004), conceptual historian Reinhart Kosellek, for example, finds that between 1770 and 1830, Jacob Grimm's

Deutsches Wörterbuch registers more than one hundred neologisms (for example: event, formation, duration, development, Zeitgeist) that qualify *Zeit*/time in a positive historical fashion. Similarly, the *Oxford English Dictionary* records the first use of "movement" for 1789; "formation" is increasingly employed after 1830; "duration" takes off in the early eighteenth century; "development" is unknown before 1750; and "epoch" is recorded as a seventeenth-century invention. Kosellek also links the rapid creation of "-ism" terms with "time" per se becoming a dynamic and historical force: Immanuel Kant coins "republicanism," which Friedrich Schlegel replaces with "democratism"; and "communism," "socialism," "liberalism," and "feminism" would soon thereafter invade the British Isles from the continent, only to be resisted by English terms using "-ism" to combat this new obsession with temporality, movement, and change, most prominently "conservatism" and, you guessed it, "medievalism." Thus, the English word "medievalism" in many ways represents a conservative insular reaction against the continental tendency of condemning and abandoning everything premodern. If France, Italy, and many German-speaking regions identified medieval culture as a usable past against which a different future could be constructed, Britain and the United States (except for a short period following the "American Revolution") imagined their countries and communities as linked to the medieval past by a unique kind of continuity. In noted contrast to the violent French Revolution, English politicians, historians, and artists enshrined the only major postmedieval revolutionary event in British history (1688) as a "Glorious," "Sensible," and "Bloodless" event; they celebrated any political and legal traditions deriving from the Middle Ages as signs of an organically and peacefully progressing commonwealth, the kind of ideological construction based on which Workman called nineteenth- and early twentieth-century medievalism a predominantly English phenomenon.[5]

Carolyn Dinshaw's decision to abandon modernity's obsession with temporality provides her with an epistemological advantage over generations of medievalists who strained to historicize every aspect of their scholarship and suppressed subjective elements in that scholarship. In fact, Dinshaw's position may be closest to that of the Boethian creator who exists in an "eternal Now." Her engagement with medieval and postmedieval subject positions and texts is simultaneous with the medieval "originals" as well as with the various moments in the reception of these "originals." History only irrupts into her narrative via the different ages during which she experiences a text or subject, but her book is very close to a divine eternal present, and does more than resolve what Paul Zumthor critiqued as early as 1980 as "the delusion which might lead one to speak of the past otherwise than on the basis of now."[6]

While many medievalists will agree that *How Soon Is Now?* offers truly innovative ways of rereading medieval and postmedieval cultures, only a small number will be able to perform, intellectually, epistemologically, and linguistically, the comprehensive queering of temporality Dinshaw achieves. Some medievalists may not adopt her post-historical approach because they believe that historicism still continues to be an essential and effective weapon in the arsenal against those who would enlist the Middle Ages in nationalist, colonialist, and racist causes. Dina Khapaeva's *Portrait critique de la Russie* (2012), for example, beautifully documents how Putin's Russia has in recent years embarked on a path towards a new feudalism, clan economy, Gothic morality, and even Gothic aesthetics. Other medievalists may find it hard to stop operating as alpha males within a masculinist Germanic (old and new) historicism. Elizabeth Scala has diagnosed this as an integral "part of the structure of fealty that holds together the field of medieval studies today," which sees any tendency to feminize, and hence destabilize, as a threat to the existing power structures in the field.[7] Again other medievalists may well dread that a move towards the inclusion of such quotidian matters as love, enthusiasm, and passion as acceptable elements of scholarly work might further weaken the already precarious situation of the humanities disciplines (and some social science disciplines) at the late modern university. They may, using the lyrics of Tina Turner's "What's Love Got to Do With it," want to be "taking a new direction," but cannot stop "thinking about [their own] protection," "scare[d] to feel this way." Politically motivated attacks that branded the Australian Research Council of Excellence for the History of Emotions as wasteful would support such concerns. The project, whose focus is on the formation, expression, and performance in Europe from ca. 1100 to 1800 and its reception in modern Australia, has clearly touched a nerve with those whose understanding of the medieval and early modern heritage would prefer a more masculinist understanding of the past, based on a desire for a more masculinist present.[8]

Notes

[1] Review of Dinshaw, *How Soon Is Now?*, in *Medievally Speaking*, January 27, 2014, http://medievallyspeaking.blogspot.de/2014/01/dinshaw-how-soon-is-now.html (accessed June 5, 2016).

[2] Wolfgang Saxon, "Norman F. Cantor, 74, a Noted Medievalist, Is Dead," *New York Times*, September 21, 2004, http://www.nytimes.com/2004/09/21/obituaries/norman-f-cantor-74-a-noted-medievalist-is-dead.html?_r=0 (accessed February 11, 2016).

[3] Cited in Kathleen Verduin, "The Founding and the Founder: Medievalism and the Legacy of Leslie J. Workman," *Studies in Medievalism* 17 (2009): 1–27 at 17.

[4] *American Literary History* 22 (2010): 758–72 at 759–60.

[5] I have summarized Kosellek's scholarship and its application to the term, "medievalism," in *"Medievalitas Fugit*: Medievalism and Temporality," *Studies in Medievalism* 18 (2009): 31–43.

[6] *Speaking of the Middle Ages*, trans. Sarah White (Lincoln: University of Nebraska Press, 1986), pp. 32–33.

[7] Elizabeth Scala, "The Gender of Historicism," in *The Post-Historical Middle Ages*, ed. Elizabeth Scala and Sylvia Federico (New York: Palgrave Macmillan, 2009), pp. 191–214 (p. 204).

[8] See Philippa Martyr, "Taken for Granted," *Quadrant*, October 1, 2012, quadrant.org.au/magazine/2012/10/taken-for-granted/ (accessed February 7, 2016). See also Philippa Maddern's response, "The Last Word: What Price Humanities Research?," *University of Western Australia News*, November 12, 2012, www.news.uwa.edu.au/201211125196/opinion/last-word-what-price-humanities-research (accessed February 7, 2016)

Chapter 2

Don't Know Much about the Middle Ages? Towards Flat(ter) Futures of Engagement

> *Don't know much about the Middle Ages*
> *Looked at the pictures then I turned the pages*
> *Don't know nothin' 'bout no rise and fall*
> *Don't know nothin' 'bout nothin' at all [...]*
>
> Sam Cooke (1960)

For the longest time I read these lines from Sam Cooke's song "Wonderful World" as a simple set of hyperbolic statements to better celebrate the unique nature of the singer's love ("But I do know that I love you ..."). Over the years, based on what I know about the field of Medieval Studies, I have come to understand these lines (as well as those about history, biology, science, and French in the song's first stanza) as a statement about who controls the research, scholarship, and teaching of the medieval past, and how those without academic degrees do not feel ownership of the knowledge-making process controlled by the academy. Consider for a moment Ben Detrick's 2013 article, "Game of Dorks: Inside the World of Medieval LARPing," published in *Maxim*, an international men's magazine sold worldwide to several million readers. Detrick surveys the activities of the Society of Creative Anachronism (SCA), an international organization devoted to the reenactment (dress, language, art, dining, combat) of the European Middle Ages, specifically some of its members' live action role-playing (hence: LARP) games. In these semi-ritualized games, participants physically portray "medieval" characters in a fictional setting, improvising their characters' speech and movements, and getting medieval on each other in "elaborate suits of armor and vests made from thick overlapping leather scales; others settle for pj bottoms, filthy Ugg boots, and helmets that resemble the reservoir tips on condoms."[9] The tenor of the article moves from incredulity to condescension, a condescension that culminates in a quoted statement by medievalist Laura Morreale, the associate director of the Center for Medieval Studies at Fordham University: "There is a tension between academic historians and SCA folks. [...] It took me 10 years to get my degree, and there's a notion that they just have to go out and live it and it's more real. But from a business perspective, we need people who are passionate about history." The immersive atmosphere at SCA events, one during which large numbers of contemporary, often well-educated adults attempt to inhabit the past, questions the distance (temporal and emotional) academic researchers have made the calling card of their work. Morreale seems willing to accept the existence of "people who are passionate about history" for the continued existence of her own profession ("business perspective"), but only as long as these "dilettantes" make no claims about the epistemological value of their engagement with medieval culture as being "more real" than that produced by those with academic degrees.

Morreale's direct and Detrick's indirect exteriorizations of affective forms of engagement with the Middle Ages exemplify an attitude constitutive of the establishing of many subjects and fields at the modern university during the second half of the nineteenth and the early twentieth century. For textual studies, literary studies, and linguistics, Jacob Grimm situated the transition from a pre-academic and extra-academic to a fully academic study of the medieval past as early as 1851, when philologists such as Karl Lachmann had begun to investigate "subjects for the sake of words," while Grimm himself remained interested in investigating "words for the sake of subjects."[10] What Grimm lamented was the narrowing of audacious intellectual thought and work on complex social issues into ever more sedulous, positivist, and socially unambitious endeavours during the academic institutionalization of the study of the past. Two decades closer to the full demarcation of the academy against amateurs, artists, dilettantes, enthusiasts, and journalists, Richard Wagner, Friedrich Nietzsche, and numerous others diagnosed that, while faculties of law, theology, and medicine remained intimately linked with the general public by producing judges, lawyers, priests, and medical doctors, scholars in the philological humanities, who made "purposeless" work their defining principle, were only intent on being "of use to themselves" and communicated with each other in "the usual citation-laden and deadly meaningless treatises."[11]

Even more than one hundred years after Wagner and Nietzsche deplored the closing of the academic mind towards the publics who had entrusted them with researching the past, Workman encountered a similar spirit of gatekeeping. During the late 1970s, he would roam the halls of Western Michigan University during the annual meetings of the International Congress on Medieval Studies (ICMS), speaking to everyone who would listen about organizing conference sections, establishing a journal, even founding an entire organization to promote the study of medievalism. Many of those who met him liked his enthusiastic conversations, his broad background in history and literature, and his wealth of humorous episodes from academe and beyond. However, few gave more than a passing thought to his projects. There was, for one, his use of "medievalism," which many recognized vaguely as a term that described the amateurish nineteenth-century interest in what had since become the venerable twentieth-century discipline of "medieval studies." (For example: the editor of the *Spenser Encyclopedia* rejected Workman's offer to contribute an entry on medievalism because to him medievalism was merely a Victorian fantasy; the marketing department of the University of Chicago Press rejected the proposal to publish his journal, *Studies in Medievalism*, because they determined that the subject had no existing audience; and the compilers of the MLA *Directory of Periodicals* refused to include "medievalism" as an acceptable descriptor for the journal.) In addition, Workman's ICMS conference badge read "Independent Scholar," and consequently suggested that little prestige and promise of future advancement could come from associating with him or his projects. In fact, being an independent scholar reminded colleagues of the menacing "pre-history" of academic medieval studies, a time against which they continued to define their own professional identity.

Thus, while Workman cherished the broad social appeal of medievalism as the all-encompassing process of (re)creating and (re)presenting the Middle Ages in postmedieval times, his desire for acceptance among academic medievalists steered him, too, towards the typical gestures indispensable to delimiting a new academic subject area from among existing ones. Many of his efforts were dedicated to distinguishing between medievalism (the re-vival of medieval culture) and romanticism and Victorianism (the survival of medieval culture), and to providing the study of medievalism with a serious academic pedigree similar to that of medieval studies. He also strove to defend the slowly growing field and its practitioners against colonializing moves of the founders of the New Medievalism (also referred to as New Philology), full-time academics at Ivy League institutions and with access to prestigious university presses, control of cohorts of doctoral students, and sway over the Medieval Academy of America that allowed them to appropriate the term without ever acknowledging his work.[12]

More recently, other medievalists and their organizations have attempted to remedy some of the weaknesses and extend the boundaries of traditional medieval studies. Perhaps the most significant example of such tendencies in the Anglo-American academy is the BABEL Working Group, whose credo is to be a non-hierarchical scholarly collective and post-institutional desiring-assemblage with no leaders or followers, no top and no bottom, and only a "middle." Membership of the group carries with it no fees, no obligations, and no hassles, and accrues to its members all the symbolic capital they need for whatever intra- and extra-institutional meanings they require. BABEL's chief commitment is the cultivation of a more mindful being-together with others who work alongside their group in the "ruined towers of the post-historical university." BABEL roams and stalks these ruins as "a multiplicity, a pack, not of subjects but of singularities without identity or unity, looking for other roaming packs and multiplicities with which to cohabit and build glittering misfit heterotopias."[13]

BABEL's "roaming packs" include academics and former academics who, hoping to build a "more present-minded medieval studies, a more historically-minded cultural studies, and a new misfit multiversity," have employed crowd funding, extra-academic publishing venues, and other alternative and cross-disciplinary practices and alliances. However, their intellectual hinterland has so far been exclusively Anglo-American, and their demiurgic polysyllabicity, which I personally find exhilarating, may present an insurmountable barrier for those amateurs who have never called the "ruined towers of the post-historical university" their home. This barrier may also exist, with some notable exceptions, for many of the essays and reviews published in *postmedieval* (the journal edited by Eileen Joy, and affiliated with BABEL), *Studies in Medievalism, The Year's Work in Medievalism, Medievally Speaking* (journals affiliated with the International Society for the Study of Medievalism), and book series such as *The New Middle Ages* (Palgrave; edited by Bonnie Wheeler), *Medievalism* (Boydell & Brewer; edited by Karl Fugelso and Chris Jones), *Classicism, Orientalism, and Medievalism* (Cambria; edited by Nickolas A. Haydock), and the dozens of monographs and essay collections published every year that sign on to the term "medievalism," negotiate its semantic space, and profit from and increase its rising currency.[14]

If for no other reason, the current state of the academy should make medievalists reconsider the degree to which we delimit or open access to the engagement with medieval culture. We have reliable indicators all around the world that the traditional academic study of the Middle Ages, after more than a century of growing and plateauing, is now on the decline. This is only in part due to nefarious political pressures and the oft-lamented corporatization of higher education. For the most part, it is because of a natural social phenomenon that happens when new fields, ideas, and methodologies reshape what and how we teach and learn. While, at least over the next five to ten years, we will still be basking in the reassuring proximity (at conferences) of thousands of others who are involved in what we do ourselves, there is a manifest discrepancy between the large number of students who request that we address their love of *Harry Potter*, *Lord of the Rings*, *Game of Thrones*, and medieval-themed video and computer games, and the decreasing number of actual medievalists hired to replace retiring colleagues.[15] In addition, it now appears that there will be fewer tenure line medievalists, and more contingent, part-time, and online medievalists in the academy, a development that will further blur the hierarchies to which we have become naturalized. Knowing what we know now about our own academic and other non-academic selves' enthusiasm for the medieval past, I think we should pursue more lasting partnerships with so-called amateurs and enthusiasts for the sake of a sustainable future engagement with medieval culture. After all, as Michael Cramer has stated about the members of the Society for Creative Anachronism, "[t]hese amateurs have often been studying their period for years, sometimes decades, sometimes for a whole life. They perform incredibly well-designed experiments in exper-imental archaeology or performance reconstruction. They are often more invested in the field, in terms of time and money, than are some tenured professors."[16] Othering or belittling them, as professional medievalists so often do, is a sign of unreflected defensiveness or the unwillingness to adapt to a world in which knowledge about the Middle Ages is no longer exclusively in the hands of those with doctoral degrees. Here are several examples of how the drawbridge can be lowered and how academics and enthusiasts may engage in productive communication about medieval culture.

About fifteen years ago, Gwendolyn Morgan, then editor of *The Year's Work in Medievalism*, requested that I serve as one of the readers for an essay submitted for consideration for publication. The essay, like much of the work submitted to the journal, was based on a paper originally presented at the 16th Annual Conference on Medievalism hosted by Buffalo State College in 2001. The author, Vincent J. Francavilla, had revised his presentation and hoped to see it accepted and published. As she told me later, Gwen Morgan had expected that I, a colleague trained as a German philologist and with previously proven exclusivist academic standards, would probably reject the short essay. However, I realized that the contribution, later published as "Heraldry: An Iconic Language," offered an attractive way of bridging a strong personal desire to connect with the Middle Ages through academic research. Francavilla, an independent scholar and dentist by profession, immediately stated the personal motivation of his research project: interested in his and his wife's family origins, he wondered how he could conjoin his general fascination with medievalia and family history by creating from scratch a family coat of arms based on medieval principles. Thus, his project was "the result of my attempt to bring an aspect of the medieval times into some relevance with my life today."[17] He then proceeded to employ cultural icon theory, the principles of heraldry (simplification, repetition, exaggeration, and repetition), etymology, and onomasiology to create his family's coat of arms, something "any family" can do: "By simply following the rules of heraldry," anyone "can produce a design and then register that design with the proper governmental authority. In the United States that body is the [...] Coast Guard."

I may immediately have "lost" most academic readers the moment they read that Francavilla referred to the Middle Ages as "medieval times," an expression also used when mentioning the beheading of Christians by ISIS terrorists: "The medieval times—I mean, we studied medieval times— not since medieval times have people seen what's going on."[18] It is very easy to dismiss anyone whose education failed to provide them with sufficient formal knowledge to adhere to the established nomenclature about historical periods. However, "Middle Ages" has never actually been as agreed upon a term as academic medievalists would like to assume: the English plural is not shared by other European languages (*Mittelalter*; *Moyen Âge*, *medioevo*); as a historical period, it has been defined not by itself, but rather by its "middle" position between the Renaissance and Classical Antiquity; the duration of the period can differ decisively based on geographic location and cultural development; and the colonizing application of the European term to non-European cultures has been widely questioned. In addition, as any quick comparison of the common uses of "Middle Ages" and "medieval times" in instruments such as the Google Ngram Viewer (https://books.google.com/ngrams) reveals, English-speaking popular culture, primary and secondary education, and the entertainment industry (*Food in Medieval Times; Daily Life in Medieval Times; A History of Engineering in Classical and Medieval Times; Economies in Medieval Times*; Medieval Times Dinner & Tournament) have maintained the term "medieval times" alongside the one promoted by academic medievalists. Is there a real qualitative difference between "medieval times" and "Middle Ages" that would entitle academics to repudiate "medieval times" in favour of "Middle Ages"?

In fact, could it be that the general public has never fully accepted (and will never fully accept) the academic distinction that medieval and Renaissance practices are more different than similar, but that medievalists' desire to enforce period distinctions, mostly based on "history of ideas" models, makes us look down on the mélange of "medieval" and "Renaissance" at North American Renaissance *faires* and in "early" music CDs as anachronistic conflations detached from historical contexts and rooted in generalized claims for an idyllic past? Could it be that the general public with its bird's-eye perspective actually diagnoses continuities that many of us with appointments in "Renaissance" or "medieval" specialty areas do not want to recognize? Do these irreverent publics perhaps confirm, without appropriate footnotes and degrees, what established scholars have claimed: that the modern concept of the Middle Ages is an invention that served post-1789 national ideologies in education and historiography (Jacques Heers, *Le Moyen Âge: une imposture*, 1999); that "medieval" practices persisted long after the usual event-based period boundaries of 1453, 1485, 1492, 1516, etc., in a *longue durée* (Fernand Braudel, *Les rois thaumaturges*, 1924) into the late eighteenth and early nineteenth century; and that the "middleness" of the period was little more than an "amoebic construct justified by nothing firmer than the uneven thinning out and eventual demise of Roman provincial government in Western Europe for a beginning, and, at the other end, the self-congratulating pronouncements of a few Italian intellectuals" who maintained they "definitely wrote better Latin than anyone who had lived since Cicero"?[19]

The second feature traditional medievalists will reject within Francavilla's short essay is the ahistorical motivation for his project, a presentist stance that openly rejects the alterity they consider a precondition for the foundation and continuation of medieval studies as an academic field. Instead of the *sine ira et studio* with which nineteenth-century scholars in the humanities and social sciences demarcated their academic subject status from their dangerously unscholarly Romantic and Victorian precursors, Francavilla assumes that it makes little sense to engage with medieval culture without reliving or actualizing it in some way. His stance does not negate the historicity of the practices and artefacts he considers, but it presupposes the possibility of a common humanity accessible to everyone across centuries.

My second example about how to reconnect non-academic amateurs with academic lovers of the Middle Ages involves the participation of several hundreds of thousands of "medievalists" every year. In 1996, an idiosyncratic French lover of the past by the name of Michel Guyot decided to purchase a piece of land near Treigny in northern Burgundy, and to build on this site a medieval castle from scratch. Since 1997, and probably at least through 2030, more than seventy craftsmen and -women (among many previously long-term unemployed) have been and will be building before many spectators' eyes a medieval castle, strictly following thirteenth-century techniques. The natural site in the middle of a dense forest provides them with all the building material necessary: wood, water, stone, earth, sand, and iron. Quarriers, stonemasons, woodcutters, carpenter-joiners, blacksmiths, tile makers, carters, and rope makers work exactly as they once did during the rule of French King Philip Augustus; other participants may join to assist them for internship-like stays as long as they are at least sixteen years old, have "a positive attitude," are "in good health," and speak French. The construction site is located five miles from the nearest village, twenty miles from the nearest railway station, and without any link to public transportation. The goal is maximum authenticity in every technology implemented, with contemporary French workers' security (health and safety) legislation as the only limiting factor.[20]

Since this new medieval castle is built in a place that did not hold a historical one, the project cannot claim any quasi-synchronicity with medieval times related to the building site itself. Instead, it derives its memorial powers from the deep sense of authentic imitation and assimilation that connects twenty-first century workers and architects with their medieval counterparts, their work ethic, sense of time, outward appearance, and even behaviour. As one visitor described the atmosphere:

> From the moment I leave the jarringly modern reception area, it really does feel like going back in time. Horse-drawn carts clatter past with timber from the surrounding woods. Staff workers in full 13th-century costume—there are about 70 of them—wander between huts carrying items such as lump hammers and hemp bundles. Practically everything here, in fact, is made on site, from ropes and saws to roof tiles. Overlaying it all, meanwhile, is the chink, chink, chink of the masons. Locals call it "the music of Guédelon"—the constant reverberation of iron on stone as new blocks are fashioned for a castle that keeps growing.[21]

And just like in Google's headquarters in Mountain View, California, whose grass-trimming herds of goats are supposed to invoke the feel of a carefree premodern farming community in the context of "clean" twenty-first-century technology, animals in Guédelon are allowed to roam freely.

Michel Guyot's castle Guédelon may well be the most large-scale effort ever at bridging the temporal chasm between the medieval past and the present to remain integrated in our collective past through replicating it within as realistic a maker culture as possible. A staggering three hundred thousand visitors, from individuals to large school classes, have been joining the builders in the active remembrance of the medieval past every year. These visitors not only testify to the continuing strong interest in medieval culture, but also prove wrong the prophecies of doom and derisive reactions Guyot and his collaborators originally received from those who could only see amateurish "enthusiasm" and futile "folly" in a project that seemed to revert back to the days before most societies transferred the task of engaging with the Middle Ages to professional students of art, culture, history, language, and literature.[22]

However, academic and non-academic "lovers" of medieval culture realized early on in the project that they needed a symbiotic approach from which both could profit. A group of academics, mostly from the fields of architecture (specifically castellology) and art history, have accompanied the construction of the castle as members of an academic advisory board, providing expert knowledge based on their research on other castle sites and historical sources on medieval building practices. In return, the makers of Guédelon have shared with scholars what they have been learning by actually practicing the techniques described in medieval manuscripts, offering invaluable original infor-mation about the realities and duration of all aspects of castle planning and construction. In this symbiotic approach in reverse archaeology (discovery by building above ground, not by unearthing ruins), reenacting makers and academic researchers are true partners. Scholars and makers even agreed that it would add to the realistic framework, and therefore to the scientific validity, of the project to invent a fictitious owner for the castle, one Seigneur Guilbert Courtenay, aka Guilbert de Guédelon, "a middling lord, with youngish children," and to determine the castle as "a new-build, small residential castle to a common late twelfth- and early thirteenth-century design, commissioned in 1228."[23] As a leader of his imagined rank and moderate income, for example, he can afford to build only a modest castle, without a moat or many architectural refinements.

The mutual respect and appreciation between those who tend to love the Middle Ages as enthusiastic makers and those who have sublimated that love into meticulous scholarly study has inspired artisans (www.newyorkcarver. com/guedelon.htm) as well as scholars already involved with connecting the general public with the past (the BBC's 2014 five-episode *Secrets of the Castle* "factual television" series) to further extend the project's reach. Anne Baud, a professor of archaeology at the University of Lyon and member of Guédelon's academic advisory board, best expresses the incredible value this non-academic approach affords her work: "My usual job is to do research on the walls [...]. In fact we mentally deconstruct the wall under investigation. This goes pretty far, but remains cerebral. Today, the work site of Guédelon helps us to implement ideas as well as research."[24] The opportunity to apply the usually entirely cerebral academic study of medieval structures to a concrete practice of reenacting construction has recently attracted scholars at France's Institut national de recherches archéologiques préventives (Inrap), a state-funded association dedicated to preserving the country's national archaeological heritage. Not only has Inrap funded the production of a ninety-minute documentary, with the tongue-in-cheek title *Guédelon: la renaissance d'un château médiéval* (ARTE France, Inrap, Lion Television, 2014), but it has also extended Guédelon's collaborative teaming up of theory and practice towards the (re)construction of a working water mill. According to Gilles Rollier, an Inrap medievalist, the project's great advantage is that "by confronting the theory, assumptions from excavations, and the reality of construction allows us to understand the skills of medieval craftsmen."[25] Thus, the result is the very authenticity scholars have claimed would be compromised by mixing the inhabiting of medieval culture with distanced academic research. In fact, the collaborative reconstitution of the entire castle as well as the water mill is a form of critical making, and it produces the kind of research opportunity medievalists have only been able to dream about in science fiction.

How unthinkable this dream of authenticity was for scholars before Guyot's Guédelon is revealed in Michael Crichton's 1999 novel *Timeline*. Crichton's narrative, which is deeply indebted to traditionalist scholarly epistemologies as well as Norman Cantor's *Inventing the Middle Ages* (1991), has to invoke quantum transportation between multiverses to send a group of archaeologists back to the medieval past. When Chris Hughes, one of the Yale graduate students at the archaeological site, time travels to 1357 France, he is finally able to resolve some of the wicked questions to which his traditional scientific scholarship on fortified mill bridges had never yielded more than approximations.

Crichton celebrates this moment of otherwise ever-elusive absolute eyewitness authenticity:

> His attention was drawn to the right, where he looked down on the great rectangular complex of the monastery—and the fortified mill bridge. *His* fortified bridge, he thought. The bridge he had been studying all summer—And unfortunately looking very different from the way he had reconstructed it in the computer.[26]

Based on his immersion with traditional medieval studies, Crichton understands that medievalists are driven by a strong desire for presenting as authentic a pastist picture of medieval culture as possible. As such, they despise popular simplifications of their scholarly interests and loathe the commodification and consumerization that would suggest a presentist relevance for the subject of their investigations. At the Guédelon project, these traditional boundaries and hierarchies have flattened into a balance more in sync with the general flattening of knowledge reception and production brought about by technology and global connectivity. Non-academic lovers of the Middle Ages involved at Guédelon no longer feel that they "don't know much about the Middle Ages" but, as artisans, reenactors, workshop and internship participants, and even as consumer–visitors, they contribute actively to the contemporary knowledge production about medieval culture. Thus, the Guédelon experiment is expanding and equalizing access to a deep engagement with the medieval past similar to those practicing the medieval art of blacksmithing, reenacting the Battle of Hastings, and performing medieval dance, theatre, and music.[27]

Obviously, not all medievalists can enjoy working on a project involving experimental architecture (Guédelon's US "mirror project," the Ozark Medieval Fortress in Lead

Hill, Arkansas, failed in 2012 after a four-year trial period). However, academic medievalists can write for more than one audience. Some of us are able to follow the example of scholar Umberto Eco, who not only wrote a scholarly book on the aesthetics of Thomas Aquinas, but also touched a larger public with his essays on the afterlife of the Middle Ages in major newspapers and his worldwide bestseller *The Name of the Rose* (1986). More recently, there is Bruce Holsinger, author of two learned studies about medievalism (*The Premodern Condition: Medievalism and the Making of Theory*, 2005; *Neomedievalism, Neoconservatism, and the War on Terror*, 2007), but also of two successful historical thrillers (*A Burnable Book*, 2014; *The Invention of Fire*, 2015) that invite readers to the era of Geoffrey Chaucer, Richard II, and the early decades of the Hundred Years' War.

However, non-academic medievalists can contribute similarly enthralling retellings of medieval narratives and often demonstrate even more forcefully the impossibility of reading a medieval text without being influenced by that text's history of reception. For example, in *Siegfried und Krimhild* (2002), a retelling of the Middle High German *Song of the Nibelungs* (*Nibelungenlied*), German writer and TV journalist Jürgen Lodemann employs various continuist strategies (etymology; neologism; toponymy; typography; mélange of narrative and scholarly commentary), to reveal how Germany's calamitous political history during the late nineteenth century and the first half of the twentieth century can be seen to be prefigured by the actions and decisions situated in the medieval epic. Specifically, Lodemann sees the unholy trinity of militant Christianity, relentless protocapitalist greed, and uncritical obedience to state authority as the foundational elements of the modern

German nation state. If Umberto Eco's postmodern interplay of fact and fiction in *The Name of the Rose* baffled traditional medievalists, Lodemann inverts many of the cultural and linguistic medievalisms employed by the second and third German Reichs to expose that even the most allegedly disinterested philological and pastist historical scholarship was more often than not in the service of an academic expansionism that accompanied dreams of military and economic imperialism. In his epic counter-mythography of 886 pages, Siegfried is no longer imperial Germany's Ur-hero, but signifies a bright and shining chance for a different, more peaceful German(ic) historical path, a path not taken because the youthful warrior is murdered by Hagen, the Burgundian ruling family's most powerful vassal. Hagen's unquestioning loyalty to his leaders heralds, in Lodemann's version, the blind and calamitous oath of personal loyalty (in German commonly referred to as "Nibelungentreue," that is, "Nibelung loyalty") that German soldiers and civil servants had to swear to Adolf Hitler (instead of the German constitution). Lodemann's openly revisionist novel affords an effective counterweight against nationalist readings of the *Nibelungenlied* that have doggedly resisted academic démentis in German-speaking political and educational settings since the late nineteenth century.[28]

If a journalist and writer like Lodemann can help raise the general reading public's consciousness of the fickle reception history of a medieval text, increasing numbers of medievalists have begun to promulgate academy-informed but broadly accessible research on medieval culture in the mainstream and social media. There is ample opportunity for informed medievalist intervention when the French right wing Front National appropriates Jeanne D'Arc (since the 1980s), when director Ridley Scott (*Robin Hood*, 2010), New Hampshire state legislators (2015), and the British Museum (2015 exhibit *Magna Carta: Law, Liberty, Legacy*) find themselves inspired by "our" Magna Carta, when British politicians seriously consider fighting contemporary jihadism with a late medieval treason law (2014), when Australian Prime Minister Tony Abbott appoints Prince Philip to a knighthood of the Order of Australia (2015), or when an all-terrain mud run in North Dakota attracts participants by calling it "Medieval Rush" (medievalrush.com; 2016). Other public outreach projects might imitate the "Medieval Baltimore" digital media history project at Towson University (medievalbaltimore.net), an effort meant to help students and a larger Baltimore audience read, critique, and appreciate the traces of medieval culture in the architecture, cultural rituals, entertainment, language, objects, and politics of their own backyard. And Sandra Alvarez and Peter Konieczny's widely received *Medievalists.net* and *The Medieval Magazine*, and my own review journal, *Medievally Speaking* (medievallyspeaking.blogspot.com) celebrate a joyous hybridity of topics, approaches, and genres of communication that invites academic and non-academic lovers of the Middle Ages to share information and learn together.

In the following chapters I will present three concise case studies of medievalism that are related to the region in which I was born and educated ("Residual Medievalisms in Eastern Bavaria"), the city in which I currently reside and teach an undergraduate course entitled "Medieval Atlanta" ("Race and Medievalism at Atlanta's Rhodes Hall"), and a central area in the reception of medieval culture more often than not avoided by academic medievalists ("Medievalism, Religion, and Temporality"). Each of the chapters is meant as an example of the kind of intervention I imagine other colleagues might also consider undertaking, interventions that would in my view reconnect the academic and non-academic engagement with the medieval past and its continuing presence in meaningful ways.

Notes

9 www.maxim.com/entertainment/game-dorks-inside-world-medieval-larping (accessed April 7, 2016).

10 "Rede auf Lachmann," in Jacob Grimm, *Kleinere Schriften, 1: Reden und Abhandlungen* (Berlin: Dümmler, 1864), pp. 145–62.

11 Richard Wagner, "An Friedrich Nietzsche," *Norddeutsche Allgemeine Zeitung,* June 23, 1872, pp. 296–302.

12 Workman summarized his efforts in a detailed interview, "Speaking of Medievalism," in *Medievalism in the Modern World: Essays in Honour of Leslie J. Workman,* ed. Richard Utz and Tom Shippey (Turnhout: Brepols, 1998), pp. 433–49. See also his review of *Medievalism and the Modernist Temper,* ed. R. Howard Bloch and Stephen G. Nichols (1996), for *Arthuriana* 7 (1997): 161–63.

13 These and the following quotes can be found at multiple Babel sites: www.siue.edu/babel/Babel-Home.htm; blogs.cofc.edu/babelworkinggroup/babelcredo/, and www.inthemedievalmiddle.com/2011/07/just-get-yourself-high-join-babel.html (accessed April 17, 2016).

14 WorldCat (www.worldcat.org/), the world's largest online library catalogue, lists seventy-nine book publications (including doctoral dissertations) that contain the term "medievalism" in their title between 1900 and 1978 (the year before the first issue of *Studies of Medievalism* was published). For 1979 through 2016, WorldCat lists 342 such titles (accessed April 16, 2016).

15 So the summary ("MAA News—From the Executive Director: 'Compatible Careers' and the Future of Academia") by Lisa Fagin Davis, executive director of the Medieval Academy of America, of the discussion at the organization's 2015 annual meeting, www.themedievalacademyblog.org/maa-news-from-the-executive-director-compatible-careers-and-the-future-of-academia/ (accessed February 14, 2016).

16 Michael A. Cramer, "Reenactment," in *Medievalism: Key Critical Terms,* ed. Elizabeth Emery and Richard Utz (Cambridge: Brewer, 2014), pp. 207–14 at 207.

[17] Vincent J. Francavilla, "Heraldry: An Iconic Language," *The Year's Work in Medievalism* 16 (2001): 107–23. Available electronically at, sites.google.com/site/theyearsworkinmedievalism/all-issues/16-2001 (accessed April 17, 2016).

[18] Cited, for example, in *salon.com* on February 8, 2016, www.salon.com/2016/02/08/donald_trump_endorses_beheading_robotic_marco_rubio_self_implodes_and_the_gop_insanity_only_gets_wilder/ (accessed April 17, 2016)

[19] Nancy Partner, "Did Mystics Have Sex?", in *Desire and Discipline: Language and Sexual Difference in Middle English Literature*, ed. Jacqueline Murray and Konrad Eisenbichler (Toronto: University of Toronto Press, 1996), pp. 296–311 at 296–97.

[20] All basic information about the castle is available at: www.guedelon.fr (accessed May 3, 2016).

[21] Olly Grant, "A Trip Back in Time at Gu[é]delon Castle," *Daily Telegraph*, November 18, 2014, www.telegraph.co.uk/travel/destinations/europe/france/Burgundy/Features/Guedelon-visitor-guide-Secrets-of-the-Castle/ (accessed May 3, 2016).

[22] This spirit of attempting something "foolish" and "amateurish" is even present in Guyot's and his collaborators' own statements about the project. See Philippe Minard and Françoise Folcher, *Guédelon: des hommes fous, un château fort* (Minerva: Aubanel, 2003).

[23] John Lichfield, "It's Now 1245, and the Walls of Guédelon are Rising," *The Independent*, September 13, 2014, www.independent.co.uk/news/world/europe/it-s-now-1245-and-the-walls-of-gu-delon-are-rising-9731564.html (accessed May 4, 2016).

[24] Minard and Folcher, *Guédelon*, p. 130 (my translation).

[25] Cited in Denis Sergent, "À Guédelon, des archéologues reconstituent un moulin du Moyen Âge," *La Croix*, May 26, 2014, www.la-croix.com/France/A-Guedelon-des-archeologues-reconstituent-un-moulin-du-Moyen-Age-2014-05-26-1156192 (my translation) (accessed May 3, 2016).

[26] *Timeline: A Novel* (1999; New York: Ballantine, 2013), p. 183.

[27] As just one recent example of such efforts I would like to mention the 2013 event, "Medievalism and Music: Das Mittelalter zwischen historisch-kritischer Aufführungspraxis und Rockkonzert," at the University of Freiburg, http://portal.uni-freiburg.de/historische-lebenswelten/veranstaltungen/Medievalism_Music/Medievalism_Music_Symposium (accessed June 7, 2016).

[28] See Richard Utz, "Jürgen Lodemann's Neo-Nibelungs," forthcoming in issue 2 of *postmedieval*, 7: *After Eco: Novel Medievalisms*, ed. Bruce Holsinger and Stephanie Trigg (2016): 289–92.

Chapter 3

Intervention One: Residual Medievalisms in Eastern Bavaria

In his 2015 study, *Medievalism: A Critical History*, David Matthews proposes that, after a period of modernity during which medievalism appeared in some of the central cultural practices in the western world, much of the medievalist energy and excitement visible in canonical texts, architecture, and the arts gradually diminished from this general domain and concentrated around the various institutionalized forms of inquiry of medievalia at the modern university. As a result, medievalism was displaced from the central cultural position it held during Britain's Victorian or America's pre- and post-Civil War periods to an increasingly marginal one. Matthews declares that this move to the margin ironically rendered medievalism almost omnipresent, albeit in smaller doses and with lesser consequence. Matthews terms this kind of medievalism "residual," remarking how medievalism now left its mark no longer with the lead genres, authors, and texts of its time as in the works of Alfred Tennyson, Walter Scott, William Morris, and Thomas Carlyle, but as mere substrates, implications, and references as in James Joyce, D. H. Lawrence, T. S. Eliot, or Ezra Pound, or as mere tropes in twentieth-century genre fiction by Umberto Eco, John Fuller, and Barry Unsworth. Similarly, Matthews expounds, there are no English-language medievalist movies that have achieved both popularity and won sufficient cultural capital to be thought of as canonical.

Matthews has a point: it is during the nineteenth century (peaking between the 1850s and the 1870s) that the study of medieval texts and art progressively passes from the hands of antiquarians, bibliomaniacs, dilettantes, and enthusiasts into those of university-educated specialists; and it is during the nineteenth century that movements like the English Medieval Revival or the French Catholic Revival dominate certain subsections of cultural production; and it is also during the nineteenth century that terms such as "medieval," "Middle Ages," and "medievalism" enter into the vocabulary of those numerous scholars who would now historicize the past. However, as I was reading Matthews's chapter, I could not rid myself of the impression that the distinction between "central" and "residual" medievalism he is writing into existence is mostly a function of his tacit agreement with the theory that, at least by the end of the "Great War," the acceptance and adaptation of medieval ideas and teleologies became too complex, if not downright impossible. Following Michael Alexander and Alice Chandler, he confirms that medievalism had a "boom" in the nineteenth century, that it "had lost its vitality before the lives of its remaining practitioners came to an end in the 1890s" (121). According to Matthews, then, the aftermath of this boom is the reason why J. R. R. Tolkien created an "infantilized" version of the Middle Ages, often "on the edge of bathos" and "about the lives of satirically small people" in *The Lord of the Rings* and *The Hobbit* instead of the serious epic and "high-art vision" of English mythology he intended to write (138). The end of the "boom" can also be seen in T. S. Eliot's

Waste Land which, while beholden to the Arthurian legend, also draws on Sophocles, Ovid, the Bible, Shakespeare, Donne, Baudelaire, and Verlaine. Another example is the painter J. W. Waterhouse, a late pre-Raphaelite whose work shows clear indebtedness to various medievalist themes. However, as Matthews underlines, he is just as indebted to classicist, Biblical, and orientalist themes and fascinated, like many late Victorian painters, not only with medieval history, but "with history itself" (121). Matthews summarizes:

> The general tendency [...] is one in which medievalist art forms have fallen outside normative canons of value and medievalist art has not regained the distinction conferred on it in the mid-Victorian period. The canonical status achieved for medievalism in that period in the spheres of art, architecture, and poetry was [...] an exception—in Britain at least, it was medievalism's bright shining moment. Subsequently, medievalism was transmuted by modernist poetry, and it is perhaps in contemporary poetry more than anywhere else that its high-art ambitions are fulfilled today: in the verse of Seamus Heaney and Geoffrey Hill, for example, and the creative translations and adaptations (in the wake of Heaney's *Beowulf*) of Simon Armitage (*Sir Gawain and the Green Knight, the Alliterative Morte Arthur*, with *Pearl* to follow) and Lavinia Greenlaw (*Troilus and Criseyde*). (138–39)

What is most surprising about this passage is not Matthews's undisputable claim of a boom time for medievalist activity in art, architecture, and poetry during the mid-Victorian era, but that he seems to posit what he calls medievalism's "high-art ambitions" as the measuring rod for its centrality or marginality. Matthews does admit that "medievalism outlasted modernism and adapted, eventually to take the place it currently holds in postmodern popular culture, where its presence in a range of cultural forms today is easy to detect—especially in films, computer games, graphic novels, music (from folk to heavy metal), heritage and tourism" (122).

If I did not know Matthews's previous work, I could very easily read this passage as suggesting that medievalism can only ever be said to be central to a culture when that society's cultural elite is involved in originating medievalist works of art. The way Matthews describes the lower-level remnants of medievalism's Victorian "boom," postmodern popular culture sounds dangerously close to what Hans Naumann once defined as "gesunkenes Kulturgut," the kind of low-brow and merely imitative borrowing or copying by socially inferior strata of superior and original cultural productions springing from the upper social strata and intelligentsia. Naumann's theory, which originates out of folklore studies right after the end of the nineteenth century, looked down on such borrowings as ignorant and "degenerated" misunderstandings of their superior models.[29]

Nothing could be further from Matthews's mind. He mentions in his study that he has gleaned his specific semantics of "residual" from Raymond Williams's *Marxism and Literature*. Based on Williams's keywords, "medievalism may be," so Matthews, "within a given phase of a culture, dominant, emergent, or residual," "a cultural formation 'effectively formed in the past, but ... still active in the cultural process, not only and often not at all as an element of the past, but an effective element of the present'" (19). Channelling Williams further, Matthews states that he is specifically interested in whether "this residual cultural element has an 'alternative or even oppositional relation to the dominant culture,' or whether it 'has been wholly or largely incorporated into the dominant culture'" (19). He then suggests that medievalism's impact in any culture might actually be at its most pervasive when it is residual, i.e. fragmented but omnipresent, rather than dominant, i.e. central and canonical, but limited to the social and intellectual elite.

In what I would like to see as a medievalist intervention in the traditions in the region in which I was born, raised, and educated, I want to complicate Matthews's observations by confronting them with medievalisms occurring in cultural contexts substantially different from the British framework informing his study. Medievalisms in the geographical area comprising post-1871 Germany include various and well-known nationalist and nativist incarnations. However, due to the long-term particularist histories dominating the German-speaking world, regional folk customs, often linked with religious traditions, co-exist alongside the more generally known national medievalist discourse from the late nineteenth century more than into the first half of the twentieth century. These regional histories, often rooted in the medieval past, are not always easily traceable, but often continue as thought patterns, mentalities, and rituals that resist even the most radical social and political upheavals, including two world wars and their accompanying pervasive social and political changes.

Several times every week, I speak with my mother back in Germany via FaceTime. At the age of eighty-eight, she suffers from any number of age-related health issues, but all of them seem to be exacerbated by abrupt changes in weather conditions. One of the issues she will mention at least once every month is a weather condition she variously calls the *Ostwind* (Easterly wind) or *der Böhmische* (short for the Bohemian wind) which, whether by changing barometric pressure or the electrification of the atmosphere, she blames for a deterioration in her symptoms, including high blood pressure and severe backaches. What I find fascinating about her attribution of these instances of deterioration is that they always originate from a vague eastern origin and that they seem to invoke, in her voice and my own reception, a deeper and darker danger that is part of an ineffable but nevertheless traceable collective memory my mother, her neighbours, and many inhabitants of her region share. Above and beyond its existence as a scientifically established weather pattern, a katabatic wind similar to the Adriatic *bora* or the Californian *Santa Ana* winds, the "Bohemian" or "Easterly" wind seems to be a cultural as well as a meteor-ological phenomenon. As a cultural phenomenon, it stands for a century-long fear of foreign invasions from the East.

I participated in this narrative of vague fear of the East when serving in the German army as an eighteen year old, stationed in a garrison securing the German border towards Communist Czechoslovakia. Unlike Sarah Palin, we really could see the Russian tanks across no-man's-land only a few miles away. During this military service, I was "volunteered" to participate as a lay actor, dressed in a medieval soldier's garb, in what may well be Germany's oldest continuing open-air folk pageant, the City of Furth im Wald's *Drachenstich* (*Spearing of the Dragon*; www.drachenstich.de). Similar to the medieval Corpus Christi procession from which today's pageant and play originate, my fellow soldiers and I would walk through the streets of the city centre performing fake sword fights. The play itself features a romantic story of a brave knight who saves a damsel in distress by killing a dragon. This dragon, representing the incarnation of evil, is symbolic of a never-fully-explained threat of ravaging war from the dark border forests of the East and perhaps related to the teachings of the church reformer Jan Hus, and it reminds viewers of the dragon speared by St. George.

The version of the play performed in 1932 was written by a man by the name of Eugen Hubrich (1885–1963), a teacher, teacher educator, and active member of the Bayerische Wald-Verein (1883–), an association celebrating and creating regional identity and advocating for economic support for the relatively poor population in the Bavarian borderlands. Already prior to Hitler's takeover of power, Hubrich had published poetry that contained the ingredients of the borderland ideology and stressed the sacrifice of the region's inhabitants and their role in defending German national identity. Then, in 1933, he openly advocated for the construction of refuge huts for hikers along the Czechoslovak border, calling them "Stamm- und Trutzburgen" ("family seats" and "castles constructed for the siege of an enemy castle") for "Germanity" and inviting his readers to think about ways of uniting with the Sudeten Germans living on the Czech side of the border. As the most potent unifying practice he encouraged the singing of songs that "warm the heart with German homely sounds" ("Heimatlaut").

In the same year, he published the panegyric poem "Heil Hitler," which reads (in my translation):[30] "Deep there in the Bohemian Forest, / Where people love their home, / And will give up property and life for their home, / Germany's waken-ing call turns into the cry for a saviour, / Heil Hitler today and forever, / Heil Hitler especially when there is danger." The connectivity between these texts demonstrates how effortlessly border-regional nativist identity and pseudo-Christianity (the text invokes well-known prayers of inter-cession to the Virgin Mary) could be integrated with the national–socialist glorification of a leader–saviour who would free the German nation from the eternal eastern threat of its Slavic neighbours that Hitler had mentioned as early as 1924 in *Mein Kampf*.

In 1934, on the invitation of Joseph Filbig, the Nazi mayor of Amberg who wanted to mark the 900th anniversary of the city's first recorded mention, Hubrich wrote the text for an open-air pageant entitled *Amberger Blut*. The pageant centres around the lavish wedding festivities for Margarete, daughter of Duke Ludwig IX of Bavaria, with Philip the Upright, Elector Palatine of the Rhine, in 1474, and performed in front of the late medieval Gothic City Hall. In his foreword to the play, Hubrich stylized Philip's adoptive father, Count Friedrich, as an indisputable allegorical predecessor of Adolf Hitler, a leader who unites a disjointed country, battles down unjustified bourgeois resistance, increases prosperity, keeps non-Arians out of higher education and most businesses, so that everyone can see in these medieval historical events the prefiguration (in his own words, "the dawning") of Hitler's Germany.[31] My parents, both born in Amberg, and aged thirteen and seven years in 1934, may well have been witnesses to the widely advertised events surrounding the pageant and the pageant itself. They were participants in the pageant in 1954, when the former Nazi major had become major of Amberg once again, this time democratically elected with 64 per cent of the vote as candidate for the right-wing party *Deutsche Gemeinschaft*. Like many other citizens, my parents dressed in handmade premodern garb to populate the main square, and my father, a music teacher, directed one of the choirs providing the musical portions of the performance.

In 1935, Eugen Hubrich, now advanced to the position of a NSDAP district warden for cultural affairs, wrote perhaps his most famous pageant, *Die Agnes Bernauerin zu Straubing*.

For this play and festival, the goal was again the creation of regional and national identity, in this case through the celebration of the 500th anniversary of the death of Agnes Bernauer, a fifteenth-century figure widely memorialized in Bavarian and German literature and art. Born around 1410, she is believed to have been the daughter of an Augsburg citizen, and became the lover, perhaps even the wife, of Count Albrecht III of Bavaria. The most common narrative assumes that Albrecht's father, Count Ernst, disapproved of his son's mésalliance with a woman of lower social status and had her drowned in the Danube river. One of the many Nazi messages inserted in Hubrich's version of the Agnes Bernauer story is a rebuke of Count Ernst's notion that the outcome of his son's relationship with Agnes would produce a "bastard" offspring. His son's answer is: "He who has German blood running through his veins cannot a bastard be."[32] And Agnes herself, right before her death, prophesies "Faith will live on, even if we perish," an unambiguous reference to a famous dictum ("Germany will live on, even if we perish") by Heinrich Lersch, a famous worker poet and among the eighty-eight poets and writers who vowed total obedience and loyalty to Adolf Hitler in 1933. At the premiere of the pageant in 1935, the audience sang a song referring to the Hussite danger threatening Bavaria from the East. Then the leading NSDAP regional magistrate reminded the audience of the impending Bolshevik threat from the Slavic peoples to the East. And in a 1937 performance, after the final song of the choir, a loud and joyous "Alleluja!" was replaced with the more up-to-date "Heil, Deutschland, Heil!".

Hubrich's medievalism reveals itself as a situational practice that will invoke continuity as well as discontinuity with the Middle Ages as needed to promote specific ideological goals. While he is eager to show how the contemporary Nazi rule has replaced all medieval class- and status-based privileges by a simple national affiliation based on common German "blood," he writes the following about his intentions with the pageant on Agnes Bernauer:

> To bring back to life the Castle of Straubing with its contemporary (medieval) inhabitants, to make Agnes Bernauer speak and act there as a real person, means an interweaving of destiny with the place in which the destiny happened, means the fulfillment of the word in blood and soil. The great-grandchildren should feel what their ancestors have felt in the same location. However, they should also realize how Agnes was sacrificed as a member of the Volk, devoured by the gruesome Middle Ages, but that she may be resurrected in purity at a happy moment in time, during which the renewal of blood and morals by the Volk is realized from within its deepest and earliest origins. (my translation)

The staying power of Hubrich's plays was considerably enhanced by the pageant genre for which he wrote. The participation of large numbers of citizens joining in the reenactment of the medieval and early modern historic moments, the presence of actual historical buildings serving as *lieu de mémoire*, and the inclusion of ritual and musical elements all contributed to his productions' performances long after the end of the Third Reich. *Amberger Blut* was revived during the conservative Amberg backlash against denazification in 1954, and his play about Agnes Bernauer continued to be performed in more and more expurgated versions until 1989. Hubrich remained in charge of the various revisions to the play until his death in 1963.

Hubrich spent about one year in prison for his rather central role in the NSDAP, but was allowed to take up his profession as a teacher after he served his time. He focused his postwar poetic production on non-political regional, dialectal, and religious texts. His most famous work is the text to composer Ferdinand Neumaier's composition of the *Waldlermesse* or "Mass written for [a] resident[s] of the Bavarian Forest," which is even today one of the most popular and widely sung and played public events in Eastern Bavaria. While denied the official status of a Catholic mass by the religious authorities, it is most often performed during events happening at the interstices of official Catholic ritual and secular, often folksy, festivities. It contains no direct support for Nazi ideology, yet it is also difficult to read it as text dedicated to the Catholic liturgical tradition. However, the text seems to affect piety and suggests an almost pantheistic nature mysticism, within which God only exists as some kind of impersonal eternal principle or cosmic force.[33] Perhaps more significantly, the text, which celebrates premodern rural life and associates meaningful speech and agency with taciturn, truthful, and independent farmers surrounded by primeval forests, is indebted to the very border-country ideology that became a political program during the Weimar Republic and the Third Reich, and added cultural significance to a meteorological phenomenon, the darkly threatening Bohemian or Eastern wind. In fact, Hubrich's *Waldlermesse* and songs about the famous Bohemian wind continue to appear together on numerous Bavarian music compilations. Its reception attests to the fact that he once again created just the right tune, the "Heimatlaut" ("homely sound") he already recommended to the Sudeten Germans in the Bohemian border country in 1933.

What can we learn from this example of residual regional medievalism? Does it really matter whether residual medieval cultural elements have an alternative or even oppositional relation to the dominant culture, or have been wholly or largely incorporated into the dominant culture, as Matthews asks? This quick foray into the history of medievalist open-air pageants in Eastern Bavaria would indicate that residual medievalisms are as resistant to change as we know other mentalities and collective memories to be. As an epistemological semi-conscious, they have continued to produce meaning during the (second) German empire, the Weimar Republic, the Third Reich, the Federal Republic of Germany, and contemporary Germany. That this is possible either means that Matthews's distinction is not as relevant as he thinks it is, or, and this is my hunch, that the political and social changes between the late nineteenth century and the early twenty-first century were not as clear cut and momentous for the general population as historians of ideas would claim. This suggests to me that as intellectuals we have an ethical obligation to intervene publicly to expose ideologies that would otherwise continue unnoticed and unopposed under the guise of seductively vague invocations of the medieval past.

Notes

[29] See Hassan El-Shamy, "Gesunkenes Kulturgut," in *Folklore: An Encyclopedia of Beliefs, Customs, Tales, Music, and Art*, ed. Thomas A. Green, 2 vols. (Santa Barbara: ABC-CLIO, 1997), 1:419–23.

[30] All quotations in this section on Hubrich are taken from Albrecht Bald, *"Braun schimmert die Grenze und treu steht die Mark!" Die NS Bayerische Ostmark/Bayreuth 1933–1945: Grenzgau, Grenzlandideologie und wirtschaftliche Problemregion* (Bayreuth: Bumerang, 2004), pp. 219–22.

[31] Eugen Hubrich, *Amberger Blut: Festspiel zur 900-Jahrfeier der Stadt Amberg*, ms. Bayerische Staatsbibliothek (1934), n.p.

[32] All quotations on *Die Agnes Bernauerin zu Straubing* are based on Bald, *"Braun schimmert die Grenze und treu steht die Mark!"*, pp. 219–22.

[33] My description of the *Waldlermesse* follows the analysis by Maximilian Seefelder, "Wie erkennt man (mangelnde) Qualität? Eine Werkanalyse am Beispiel der Waldler-Messe," in *Studientagung zur Kulturarbeit in Niederbayern an der Universität Passau am 12. Juli 2003: Vier Vorträge*, ed. Patricia Mindl (Passau: University of Passau, 2004), pp. 13–26.

Chapter 4

Intervention Two: Race and Medievalism at Atlanta's Rhodes Hall

On a Saturday afternoon in September 1906, newsboys in Atlanta's Five Point neighbourhood tried to attract customers with the following headlines:

> "Extra! Third Assault on White Woman by a Negro Brute!"
> "Extra! Bold Negro Kisses White Girl's Hand!"
> "Extra! Bright Mulatto Insults White Girls!"[34]

These alleged assaults, none of which were ever substantiated, and other sensationalized headlines, stories, and cartoons appeared in Atlanta newspapers in the wake of a particularly adversarial Georgia gubernatorial race, during which both candidates, Clark Howell and Hoke Smith, two of Atlanta's most prosperous citizens and champions of white supremacy, did everything in their power to paint their opponent as being too friendly with the city's black citizens. The *Atlanta Constitution*, which Howell published, accused Smith of appointing blacks to federal positions during his time as secretary of the interior under Grover Cleveland. One of Smith's supporters, the South Georgia demagogue Tom Watson, asked his audience: "What does civilization owe to the negro?" And he answered what to him was a rhetorical question: "Nothing! *Nothing*! NOTHING!"

It mattered little that the *Atlanta Independent*, a black weekly, pointed out how both campaigns disenfranchised "every decent and helpful negro citizen and enfranchize[d] every venal and vicious white thug." Atlanta, the city that prided itself on being an exception among the racially divided cities of the South, quickly succumbed to the lurid and dramatic news hype spread by the major newspapers: "With his yellow lips forming insulting phrases," the *Evening News* exclaimed, "Luther Frazier, a young negro, attacked Miss Orrie Bryan, the pretty eighteen-year-old daughter of Thomas L. Bryan, in her home." And the journalists spurred on local men by asking: "What will you do to stop these outrages against the women? Shall these black devils be permitted to assault and almost kill our women, and go unpunished?"

As a result of this and other inflammatory rumours, white men and boys gathered all over Atlanta and attacked black-owned businesses, pulled some black men out of trams and trolleybuses, hunted others down in the streets. Long-held fears, especially of black sexual violence against white women, continued to lead to attacks by white mobs on black citizens during the following days, even after the state militia had entered the city to stop the violence. In the end, about forty African Americans were killed, along with two whites. A five-year-old white girl, named Peggy, would be traumatized profoundly when she saw her father, who did not own a gun, stand outside his front door, holding an axe and an iron water key, ready to defend her against the alleged black assailants. The girl would grow up to become Margaret Mitchell, one of the nation's first women journalists and author of *Gone With the Wind*, a novel that David O. Selznick's 1937 movie version fittingly summarized for spectators with Ben Hecht's opening intertitle:

> There was a land of cavaliers and cotton fields called the Old South. Here in this pretty world, gallantry took its last bow. Here was the last ever to be seen of knights and their ladies fair, of Master and of slave. Look for it only in books, for it is no more than a dream remembered, a civilization Gone With the Wind...

The strong medievalist ethos of the elite culture in the south of the United States epitomized in the book and film versions of *Gone With the Wind* is of course well known.[35] As Scottish and English immigrants formed the centre of European immigration to the early South, these immigrants considered themselves more British than American, and looked to Britain and British self-fashioning narratives for cultural orientation and social standards. Walter Scott's medieval novels, which romanticized the English court, captured the early Southern imagination, and so it was that the medieval knight rather than the rough American pioneer became the Southern ideal. Linking themselves to the closest contemporary archetype of the medieval knight, the British nobleman, the Southern aristocracy rebuked newer (and Northern) foreign ideologies of materialism, feminism, and pacifism because they seemed to be the antithesis of honour, valour, gentility, hospitality, and chivalry, and they celebrated their own scaled-down version of the medieval court, the Southern gentleman land and slave owner and his belle.

How deeply this medievalist ideology trickled down even into the upwardly mobile white working class can be demonstrated by looking at the career and aspirations of

Amos Giles Rhodes. Born in Henderson, Kentucky, in 1850, he came to Atlanta as a simple labourer for the L&N Railroad in 1875. He then started his own small furniture company, which would soon grow into a large furniture business and make him one of the wealthiest and most prominent citizens of the quickly growing modern city. This city, in part because of its modernity and rapid growth, offered better living conditions and career opportunities not only for whites, but also for black workers and businesses than any other city in the late nineteenth-century South. Between the 1890s and 1910, Atlanta's population soared from 80,000 to 150,000; the black population was approximately 9,000 in 1880, and it had reached 35,000 by 1900. Such rapid growth put pressure on municipal services, created increased job competition among black and white workers, heightened class distinctions, and led the city's white leadership to respond with restrictions intended to control the daily behaviour of the growing working class, with mixed success. Such conditions caused concern among elite whites, who feared the social intermingling of the races, and led to an expansion of racial segregation, particularly in the separation of white and black neighbourhoods, including separate seating areas for public transportation. Those new to Atlanta often marvel why so many thoroughfares in the city all of a sudden change names without discernible cause. The cause is, of course, as Kevin Kruse has documented, that white Atlantans have tried very hard to avoid having a "black address."[36]

On the white side of Atlanta, Amos Rhodes and his wife, Amanda, who had become enamoured with castles they had seen during a visit to the Rhineland in the 1890s, began to assemble an estate of 114 acres along one of the most highly prized Atlanta thoroughfares, Peachtree Street. In 1902, only four years before the Atlanta race riots, construction began on a large private castle, which the couple situated for maximum visibility on a slight rise at a prominent curve of Peachtree Street and called "Le Rêve," or "The Dream." The granite for the mansion was quarried twenty-five miles east of Atlanta from the same Stone Mountain that would, in 1915, become the site for the founding of the second Ku Klux Klan, and for which, also in 1915, the Daughters of the Confederacy would commission a carving of the Confederate icons Robert E. Lee, Thomas "Stonewall" Jackson, and Jefferson Davis.

By the time Rhodes Hall was built, the Rhineland castle style was already out of fashion, and architect Willis F. Denny II (1874–1905), who also designed Atlanta's First United Methodist and St. Mark's United Methodist churches in the style of the popular Gothic revival, created an example of Victorian Romanesque Revival, which was intended to adapt the medieval Romanesque style to the design of a twentieth-century home. As so often in modern medievalism, the Victorian Romanesque Revival typically made only super-ficial reference to the actual architecture of the medieval period. The style, exemplified by San Francisco's St. Mark's Lutheran Church (1895), Chicago's Marshall Field Wholesale Store (1887), and Sydney's Queen Victoria Building (1898), featured buildings of substantial weight and mass; a rock-faced foundation; masonry walls highlighted by rock-faced arches, lintels, and sills; semicircular arches in windows, doors, and porches; polychrome masonry; and tower roofs topped with a hip know and/or finial.

Due to its massive and expensive construction require-ments, the style was typically employed for grand, public buildings such as courthouses, churches, libraries, university buildings, department stores, and train stations. Rhodes Hall, which cost the Rhodes family $50,000 to build in 1904 (in today's currency, this would be at least $1.2 million, and perhaps as high as $29 million), is a notable exception to this general picture. According to contemporary records, the house was an immediate success in the Atlanta papers and social scene. In fact, one author has stated that "in the war of wealth and opulence waged along Peachtree Street at the time, it can probably be said that Amos Rhodes's fortress won hands down."[37] And it won this "war" not only through its typically Victorian obsession of connecting with the medieval past, or its display of exotic scenes from the Rhodes's beloved Florida, but also by weaving into these temporally and spatially removed features the most advanced contemporary technology. Over three hundred light bulbs illuminated the house, producing a blaze of light still uncommon in 1904, and most rooms boasted electric call buttons as well as a security system.

At the very centre, visually and symbolically, of the castle on Peachtree is a massive mahogany staircase, which leads up to the private and much less ornately decorated areas of the Rhodes home. The staircase, for which the architect used mahogany imported from the West Indies, magically attracts a visitor's eyes to a three-panel series of stained and painted glass. It is in these panels that the owners and their architect decided to create a church-like shrine to the "Lost Cause," romanticizing the rise and fall of the Confederacy from the first shots initiating the Battle of Fort Sumter on April 12, 1861, to the Battle of Appomatox, after which General Robert E. Lee's army surrendered on April 9, 1865.

Figure 1. General Robert E. Lee saying goodbye to his soldiers before departing to sign the terms of surrender at Appomattox Courthouse.

The windows were executed by the industrious brothers Theodore and Ludwig Von Gerichten who, with studios in Columbus, Ohio, and Munich in Germany, created windows for approximately eight hundred and fifty churches in the United States and who were recognized with four gold medals at the 1904 St. Louis World's Fair.[38]

The glass panels, which vary somewhat in length because of the space they cover from the bottom to the top of the staircase, consist of two longer sections depicting recognizable seminal historical moments, for example the election of Jefferson Davis as President of the Confederate States of America (1861), dramatic battle scenes, or nostalgic scenes of the Old South, interrupted by medallion-like portraits of Confederate politicians and generals, including Pierre G. T. Beauregard (1818–1893) and Henry Hopkins (1818–1886). Each window is crowned by rounded arch illustrations of abstract national virtues, for example the Constitution, supported by Wisdom, Justice, and Moderation, or mottos and seals celebrating various Confederate states, among them Alabama's "Here we rest," a popular misprision of the meaning of the Muskogean-speaking name of the tribe, the Alabama people, after which the state was named.[39]

The panels with scenes from the Old South directly comment on the race relations in Atlanta during the first decade of the twentieth century. The numerous medievalizing gestures in Rhodes Hall conflate and conjoin the medieval and the ante-bellum past as one and the same so that the temporal distance between both historical eras is completely erased. In one painted-glass image, situated in spring or summer, a bearded patriarch with a cane stands by as his wife hugs and welcomes back their son, who wears a Confederate uniform. Their yard is romantically overgrown with ivy and other

Figure 2. A Soldier's Goodbye.

abundant flora, and an askew shutter on the Classical revival ante-bellum plantation manor, which features vaguely Ionic columns, hints at the fact that the place has seen better days.

In a second image, this one situated several years before the earlier scene, the same Confederate soldier gallantly waves goodbye to his wife, son, and daughter, who return his salutation. Playing in the dark, over on the left of this almost identical manor house and close to the shade of the trees stand six black figures in white and beige workers' clothes. They observe the departure scene without visible emotion. Their hands are at their hips or down at their sides, but their motionless and unfree status provides the symbolic

Figure 3. A Soldier's Welcome Home.

backdrop in front of which the gallant manhood and freedom of the white male hero may be performed.

If what can be inferred about Amos Rhodes's taste for the Romantic and exotic in other rooms is any indication (in another room "noble native savages" are also depicted in scenes that instrumentalize them as idealized objects of a bygone American past), he felt a deep yearning for a time when medieval knights and ladies, that is Southern gentlemen and their belles, when medieval peasants and slaves, that is African American slaves, all knew their rightful place. And so it is no surprise when the final of the three scenes from the Old South presents us with what the two white Confederate soldiers are leaving to fight and

Figure 4. Cotton Harvest.

die for, a bucolic image of two African Americans occupied with providing the economic foundation for the Southern economy and lifestyle: King Cotton. The full basket up front and the ample future yield on the healthy looking plants celebrate an agrarian and anti-industrialist economy which, if it wanted to continue to grow, also had an ever-increasing need for slave labour.

Only two generations after the American Civil War, Rhodes Hall still signified that heritage, and the race riots of 1906 indicated that African Americans in Atlanta still had a long way to go to overcome the fortress mentality that the monumental Castle of Peachtree was meant to memorialize.[40]

After Amanda Rhodes's death in 1927 and Amos Rhodes's in 1928, their children deeded the house to the State of Georgia, specifying that the property could only be used for "historic purposes." In 1930 the building opened as the home of the State Archives and functioned as such until a more modern facility was built on Capitol Avenue in 1965. In 1983 The Georgia Trust for Historic Preservation, a non-profit organization, signed a long-term lease for Rhodes Hall with the State of Georgia. Serving as headquarters for The Georgia Trust, Rhodes Hall has undergone significant restoration. The State has funded restoration of the exterior and the building's mechanical and electrical systems, while the Trust has raised private funds to restore the interior. The focal point of the interior restoration was the return of the original mahogany staircase and painted-glass windows that had been removed to the State Archives facility on Atlanta's Capitol Avenue. The staircase and windows were reinstalled in Rhodes Hall in 1990.

Nowadays, Rhodes Hall serves another fascinating medi-evalizing function. If, as Swiss cultural theorist Denis de

Rougement and others have claimed, western romantic love trickled down from the medieval ruling classes' exclusive game of "courtly love" or *fin amors* into the modern bourgeoisie and then the working class,[41] the mansion's contemporary function as one of Atlanta's favourite sites for wedding ceremonies and receptions would appear quite appropriate. Advertised by The Georgia Trust as the place where couples may experience "Cupid at the Castle" (inclusive of an officiant, professional photography services, a bridal bouquet, wedding coordinator, ceremony music, and a special champagne toast and wedding cupcakes for the bride and groom), numerous Atlantans today are eager to embrace the motley mélange of medievalism and vague old-world otherness to make their special day one to remember.

However, as much as I support The Georgia Trust's initiative of maintaining the historic building via the fees couples pay for using the Castle on Peachtree, I am shocked at their willingness to propose to African American and interracial couples to exchange vows and take wedding pictures without explaining the symbols of racial segregation and slavery-based nostalgic medievalism that are at the heart of Rhodes Hall's construction and purpose. I believe that all Atlantans deserve to know that they and their public promise to each other are being memorialized by the photographers and wedding officiants while standing against the backdrop of a group of saintly looking generals who include adamant opponents of reconstruction (Robert Toombs, 1810–1885), a Grand Wizard of the Ku Klux Klan (Nathan Bedford Forrest, 1821–1877), and the head of the Ku Klux Klan in the State of Georgia (John B. Gordon, 1832–1904). While The Georgia Trust's website for Rhodes Hall includes proud mention of the building "Going Green" in recent years, the information on its history hushes up any potentially sensitive contexts and simply focuses on Rhodes Hall's representative character for what it summarizes as Atlanta's "belle époque." Similarly, all the National Park Service can find to comment on are the building's "serenity and elegance."[42]

It is in a situation like this that a public medievalist can and should intervene to contribute to an informed citizenry aware of the manifold connections between the past and the present, and expose the potentially dark side of medievalism from underneath the "belle époque" veneer. In fact, I am convinced that an intervention like this one best honours the spirit of Amanda and Amos Rhodes's desire to have their own private castle serve "historic purposes" for many years to come. Who knows if such an intervention might not contribute to a discussion similar to the one that led to the decision in June 2016 to remove the Confederate battle flag from a 1953 stained-glass window in Washington Cathedral? In this case, not only did the cathedral leaders decide to remove a specific offensive symbol, they also decided to use the windows as the centrepiece for a series of public forums and events on questions of racism, slavery, and racial reconciliation.

Notes

[34] My summary of events, including historical quotations, is based on Gary A. Pomerantz, *Where Peachtree Meets Sweet Auburn: A Saga of Race and Family* (New York: Penguin, 1997), pp. 69–77.

[35] The most recent investigation into the medieval roots of Southern chivalry is Tyson Pugh's *Queer Chivalry: Medievalism and the Myth of White Masculinity in Southern Literature* (Baton Rouge: Louisiana State University Press, 2013).

[36] See Kevin M. Kruse, *White Flight: Atlanta and the Making of Modern Conservatism* (Princeton: Princeton University Press, 2005), p. 62.

[37] Cited according to the entry on "Rhodes Memorial Hall" by the City of Atlanta's Urban Design Commission, www.atlantaga.gov/index.aspx?page=427 (accessed April 16, 2016).

[38] On the medievalist painted- and stained-glass production by the von Gerichten brothers, see John M. Clark, *German Village Stories Behind the Bricks* (Charleston: History Press, 2015), pp. 140–43.

[39] I am indebted to Dr. John Turman, novelist and tour guide at Rhodes Hall who, on May 14, 2013, provided me with an eleven-page document, "The Rise and Fall of the Confederacy: Art Glass Windows in Rhodes Memorial Hall," which includes a detailed list of all scenes, symbols, and individuals depicted in painted and stained glass.

[40] Atlanta owes its existence to the economic need for a railroad hub that would connect the port of Savannah with the Midwest. Hence, from 1836 until 1842, the small settlement's name was Terminus, indicative of its function as the zero milepost between Savannah, GA, and Chattanooga, TN.

[41] *L'Amour et l'Occident* (1939, rev. 1956 and 1972), translated by Montgomery Belgion and published in the US as *Love in the Western World* (1940), and in the UK as *Passion and Society* (1956).

[42] www.georgiatrust.org/historic_sites/rhodeshall/; www.nps.gov/nr/travel/atlanta/rho.htm (accessed March 27, 2016).

Chapter 5

Intervention Three: Medievalism, Religion, and Temporality

In *Received Medievalisms: A Cognitive Geography of Viennese Women's Convents*, published in 2013 in Bonnie Wheeler's The New Middle Ages series published by Palgrave, Cynthia Cyrus examines the complex cultural history of the reception of women's monastic communities from the Ottoman siege of Vienna in 1529 through to the nineteenth century. Focusing mainly on Augustinian, Cistercian, Clarissan, Penitent, and Premonstratensian monastic houses, she investigates an extensive panoply of multimodal references (visual, as in cartographical plans and various pictorial representations; verbal, as in travel literature, topographies, anecdotes, and legends) and fully-fledged "foundation stories" (formal histories told to relate the origins of a specific community), to present readers with the urban–historical background for evolving attitudes towards the city's past. While the women's convents:

> lack the quaintness of the Viennese *fiaker*, they substitute their own enacted ritual of liturgy for the whirl of the waltz with its emphasis on imperial and urban pleasures. Thus, they do not partake directly in the theme of "gay Vienna." These institutions do, however, capture a sense of the Viennese past that generated its own sense of longing and belonging. The convents, as portrayed in a range of postmedieval genres,

function as easily recognizable symbols of the medieval and the spiritual ancestry of a proud city, though how they do so can vary according to narrative preference and authorial perspective. With enduring walls of stone and an ongoing presence in everyday religious life, the monasteries could stand directly for the "old" and for the "Catholic" nature of the city, skyline markers of a historical Christian past. (2)

Cyrus's project is exceptional in several ways. Firstly, it focuses for the most part on early modernity, a period in which the concept of the medieval past was yet unsettled. Thus, unlike the majority of the existing academic work in medievalism studies, she explores forms of medievalism closer to the Middle Ages itself, when much of what we today identify as the medieval may have continued without notice. Secondly, Cyrus combines the theoretical and methodological areas of literary studies, urban history, monastic studies, gender history, and topographical and cognitive geography with some of the notions central to medievalism studies: authority, dis/continuity, genealogy, Gothic, heritage, identity, nostalgia, preservation, revival, ritual, and romanticism, coming very close to what Jonathan Hsy has described as medievalism's "co-disciplinarity." This furthers a "shared intellectual and creative zone" that allows individuals or groups of people "to test the very conventions of academic disciplines and to experiment across diverse modes of artistic production."[43] Finally, while her goal is not an exhaustive exploration of the Viennese nun's religious faith, she is fully inclusive of religious and theological matters as they converge with the postmedieval cognitive geography of Vienna's women's convents.

It is the exceptional nature of this third feature of *Received Medievalisms* I would like to further consider in this chapter. Specifically, I would like to ask why, despite the obvious co-disciplinary nature of medievalism and the essential role of religion in medieval culture, so few scholars of medievalism delve into examining the enduring presence and influence of religion *per se*? Perhaps the reason is to be found with what Randy Cohen, the *New York Times* "Ethicist" blogger, has diagnosed as part of general cultural etiquette: most of us have been educated to believe that "religion, especially another person's religion, should be treated with deference or, better still, silence by nonbelievers."[44] Cohen, who holds many of his own secular political convictions on social justice as dear as others do their religious beliefs, defines the difference in the public reception towards his blogs on religious and secular matters:

> When I take up a secular question that provokes broad disagreement, I typically receive a few hundred responses by e-mail that begin: "Dear Sir, I am appalled..." When I write about religion, I cause a tidal wave. The week I rebuked an Orthodox Jewish real estate agent whose beliefs forbade his shaking the hand of a female client, I stopped counting after receiving 4,000 ferocious messages, lambasting not only my argument but my character, my appearance and my parentage: it was speculated that dogs played a part.

While it is undoubtedly true that some of us prefer to avoid conflict with those to whom our scholarship on religious topics might be anathema, there are just as many scholars of medievalism who wholeheartedly embrace their role as public intellectuals whose specific task it is to add research-based commentary to the usable medieval pasts we encounter. After all, scholars of medievalism do investigate and take positions on gender, sexuality, abortion, education, politics, and so on, positions that religious individuals find objectionable. Then again, many medievalism-ists live with more than one subject position and somehow balance an allegiance to the ideals of academic study with the mandates of religious denominations and their traditions and beliefs.

From these preliminary observations I conclude that there must be additional reasons for the avoidance of religious subject matter in medievalism, and I believe the main reason may be the radically different approaches to temporality proposed by these two ways of conceptualizing the world and the relationship between past and present.

As cultural and semantic historians have demonstrated, time itself and a consciously temporalizing perspective on all subject matter become lead indicators for the advent of modernity.[45] In fact, since the early nineteenth century, temporalization has become the central weapon in the arsenal of historicism, the thought paradigm that can not only dissect and structure the present and the past, but also guide all academic study at the modern university towards distinguishable periodicities. This process is what makes new fields in the humanities occupy intellectual territory by organizing their curricula and their hiring according to historical periods and develop as quickly as possible a course on the field's own history. Even science and technology studies—fields in which new results are expressly developed to erase older ones—offer courses on the history of their subject matter. The very same process made art and cultural historians, from the 1830s onward, abandon the vague term "antiquities" and describe that which had come before their own period and initially replace or specify it by using a more clearly defined "medieval" period and "Middle Ages" (a term later particularized into "early," "high," and "late"). Soon thereafter, the new academic specialists replace "medievalism" with "medieval studies" to wrest responsibility for researching the past away from "antiquarians" and "dilettantes," and locate it with themselves. In a parallel development, diachronic principles were made to dissect linguistic periodization.

As a byproduct of this intense and accelerated temporalization, institutionalization, and particularization, and the need for a distanced view of the past, the chasm between scholars and their subjects of investigation grew ever larger, to the point where historian Leopold von Ranke's (in)famous dictum to write history as it actually happened ("wie es eigentlich gewesen ist") came to mean that an almost insurmountable epistemological boundary had been built against anyone who sought to bridge the increasingly non-contiguous historical periods of past and the present.

Even the academic subject of "Theology" succumbed to the pressure of historicizing, establishing Church History as an essential element of its degree programs. However, these theological faculties' subject matter, "religion," conceived of "temporality" in terms diametrically opposed to those of the fully historicist rest of the academy. Consider, for example, one of the most enduring disputes in the history of Christianity: transubstantiation. A majority of Christians maintain that the person of Christ is spiritually present in the Eucharist. Roman Catholic Christians affirm what they term "real presence" of the body and blood of Christ as resulting from a change of the elements of bread and wine. Lutherans agree with them in a real eating and drinking of the body and blood of Christ, except that they define it as happening by sacramental union "in, with and under the forms" of bread and wine. Methodists and Anglicans tend to avoid the controversy surrounding the question by relegating Christ's presence to the realm of religion's mystery.

More significant than these denominations' differences is their common desire to bridge two non-contiguous points in time. At the centre of their teachings is the recognition that a congregation's celebration of the Eucharist in remembrance (anamnesis) of the Last Supper is insufficient to express the sempiternal nature of Christ and God and help believers enter into as close a union with the divinity as possible. Basic intellectual "recalling" following Luke 22:19, "Do this in remembrance of me," is reinforced through a whole host (no pun intended) of liturgical actions and formulae, all forms of ritual reenactment, that culminate in the consecration of the host by the priest. The full, final, and momentous, albeit momentary, suspension of human historicity is to be reached when the consuming of the shared bread and wine allows for a direct physical and spiritual experience. Hence, the individual believer's communion with Christ can become a living reality rather than remain a mere symbolic re-*present*-ation.

This example of the sempiternality of religion offers, I believe, a useful answer to the question why scholars of medievalism studies find it difficult to engage in a critical (and "critical" has been synonymous with "historicizing") discussion of religion. Most of us may feel comfortable with dissecting Michael Crichton's narrative device of the multiverse, which in his 1999 science-fiction novel *Timeline* enables twentieth-century scientists to experience the "real" Middle Ages by moving back and forth between two parallel historical periods. Religion, however, because it resists historicity's epistemological primacy, may remain too difficult a topic for most academic scholars, which is why they have responded to this foundational epistemological aporia in a variety of ways. Here are three examples of such different approaches.

Mette Birkedal Bruun, who teaches church history at the University of Copenhagen, has advanced the possibility of challenging historicity's primacy in her work on the seventeenth-century Cistercian reception of Bernard of Clairvaux. Discussing the biography and writings of Armand-Jean de Rancé (1626–1700), a courtier turned monk and abbot of the Cistercian monastery of La Trappe in Normandy, she offers a convincing example of his deep and direct connection with Bernard's religious teachings not as a form of historicizing "medievalism," but as a synchronistic religious act. Intent on reforming his own monastery and the entire Cistercian order, he revitalized the medieval Bernardine ideals of the love of God, the humility of the soul, and the role of obedience into his own presence without any qualms about their "fit" into his own day and age. As Bruun explains:

> To Rancé, Bernard was part of a monastic tradition that was ever potentially vibrant and alive—and accessible on a synchronic note. The constitution of the monastic genealogy [between him and Bernard] is not a matter of temporal progression but of spiritual affinity. The legitimization of the reform through constant references to Bernard is not a matter of reviving an earlier golden age but of associating his own ideals with those of this epitome of Cistercian spirituality. In other words, Rancé's project appears to be almost contra-temporal. [...] In Rancé's view, history is a discipline that belongs way out of the monastic focus (unless, he admits, one has received an unequivocal call from God to that effect!). His revitalization of Bernard is not a revitalization of the medieval monk, but of a set of ideals synchronically present.[46]

Bruun, although at a church historian's investigative distance from her religious subject matter, nevertheless acknowledges how religious belief may successfully bridge the roughly five hundred years separating Rancé from his medieval model. For her, this "contra-temporal" view should not be subjected to a historicizing perspective and, thus, should not be called an example of medievalism.

Carla Arnell, who teaches medievalism and early English literatures at Lake Forest University, explains how she manages to inhabit two apparently mutually exclusive subject positions as scholar and Christian.[47] Among her reasons for balancing the demands of academic temporality and Christian sempiternality are: a) she worships regularly out of a desire "to give thanks to the divine source of all life—what Dante calls 'the love that moves the sun and other stars'"; b) "because the formal words and music, the ritual seasons, and the constant practice of religious conformity make life beautiful"; and c) because of the "link between past and present [...], that last invisible tie religion makes possible." And she continues in a vein similar to that of many presentist scholars:

> Why say the same words over and over each Sunday, the spiritual but not religious might ask? Why not do something new and different? Why not devise one's own words? Maybe there's some value in tracing the words of those who have gone before and being reminded that, as diverse as our identities are, we share such common human experiences as childbirth, friendship, love, suffering, and death.

Arnell probably speaks for a good number of students of medievalism, especially those who find a habitat in which the paradox of historicist temporality and religion does not lead to conflict, but rather yields a rich harvest of academic study. More often than not, these colleagues are guided by the scholars who lived similarly seemingly paradoxical lives, like C. S. Lewis, and find an intellectual home in journals accepting of religious belief as part of academic discourse, like *Christianity and Literature*.

Finally, there is also space and work for those who, unlike Arnell, reveal those continuing ritual, liturgical, and cultural ties not as "beautiful," but as powerful obstacles to ending some of the religious traditions that developed when Christianity's all too human involvement with history led its members and leaders astray. In the early 1990s, Manfred Eder, then a PhD student of Catholic Church History at my *alma mater*, the University of Regensburg, brought about the interdiction of the "Deggendorfer Gnad," a more than five-hundred-year-old annual pilgrimage based on an alleged "Jewish desecration" and "miracle of the host."[48] In his dissertation, he demonstrated conclusively how late medieval citizens and clergy had colluded in fabricating the legend, and how highly effective religion-based re-*present*-ation techniques, including the annual processions, indulgences, rituals, music, plays, and similar, had so deeply and lastingly shaped the small Bavarian town's identity that it took more than two hundred years, from the first critical voices during the Enlightenment until 1992, to make it cease. The interdiction came from Bishop Manfred Müller, a full ten years after his appointment in Regensburg and twenty-seven years after the end of the Second Vatican Council, which actively encouraged Christian–Jewish reconciliation. Müller's predecessor, Rudolf Graber, had refused to concede, against better knowledge, the historical facts behind the medieval legend and rejected calls for the cessation of the annual Deggendorf pilgrimage. In 1992, when the diocese honoured his memory, Bishop Gerhard Ludwig Müller attested to Graber's "incorruptibility" in the face of an "apparently omnipotent Zeitgeist," thus praising his active contra-temporal and anti-historicist stance.[49] This appreciation closely resembles an earlier one by Cardinal Joseph Ratzinger (later Pope Benedict XVI), who had underlined Graber's resistance against "the winds of time," which in his view are "really the winds of Satan," in a homily on the occasion of Graber's 60th priesthood jubilee.[50] Perhaps it is helpful to mention that Graber was responsible for Ratzinger's original 1968 appointment to a chair in Dogmatic Theology at the University of Regensburg, a position he specifically redefined from one originally slated for an appointment in Judaic Studies. We come full circle.

To me, these examples leave no doubt that medievalists have an ethical obligation to investigate and historicize religion and theology, at least in all its omnipresent temporal manifestations or in its specific attempts at contemporaneanizing the Catholic Church, as in the Second Vatican Council's initial spirit of "aggiornamento" (1962–65).

Notes

43 Jonathan Hsy, "Co-disciplinarity," in *Medievalism: Key Critical Terms*, ed. Elizabeth Emery and Richard Utz (Cambridge: Brewer, 2014), pp. 43–51 at 43.

44 ethicist.blogs.nytimes.com/2009/10/27/can-we-talk-about-religion-please/?_r=0 (accessed August 1, 2014).

45 See Richard Utz, "Coming to Terms with Medievalism," *European Journal of English Studies* 15 (2011): 1–13, for a detailed discussion of this claim.

46 For example: "A Case in which a Revitalization of Something Medieval Turned out not to be Medievalism," special issue of *UNIversitas* 2: *Falling into Medievalism*, ed. Anne Lair and Richard Utz (2006), www.uni.edu/universitas/archive/spring06/mettebruun.htm (accessed 10 May, 2016).

47 Carla Arnell, "An Academic Among the Pews," *Chronicle of Higher Education*, October 14, 2013, chronicle.com/article/Dont-Eschew-the-Pew/142241/ (accessed May, 14, 2016).

48 Manfred Eder, Die *"Deggendorfer Gnad": Entstehung und Entwicklung einer Hostienwallfahrt im Kontext von Theologie und Geschichte* (Passau: Passavia, 1992).

49 "Die Kirche von Regensburg gedenkt Bischof Dr. Rudolf Grabers," Diocese of Regensburg, January 31, 2010, www.bistum-regensburg.de/news/die-kirche-von-regensburg-gedenkt-bischof-dr-rudolf-grabers-un-bestechlich-gegenueber-der-scheinbaren-allmacht-des-zeitgeistes-1582/ (accessed May 10, 2016).

50 Cited by R. J. Werner, "Anmerkungen zum geschichtstheologischen Opportunismus bei Rudolf Graber," *haGalil.com: Jüdisches Leben online*, July 20, 2011, www.hagalil.com/archiv/2011/07/20/graber/ (accessed May 10, 2016).

Chapter 6

Manifesto:
Six (Not So) Little Medievalisms

> I had been concerned with the problem of Action, the oldest
> concern of political theory, and what had always troubled me
> about it was that the very term I adopted for my reflections
> on the matter, namely, *vita activa*, was coined by men who
> were devoted to the contemplative way of life and who
> looked upon all kinds of being alive from that perspective.
> Hannah Arendt, *The Life of the Mind* (1971)

Based on my thoughts in the previous chapters, here are
my recommendations for the future of our engagement with
medieval culture:

Manifesto One

Medievalism is the ongoing and broad cultural phenomenon
of reinventing, remembering, recreating, and reenacting the
Middle Ages. Medieval Studies, the academic study of medieval
culture focused on establishing the "real" Middle Ages, is one
essential contributor to the cultural phenomenon of Medievalism.
As Kathleen Verduin once stated: "[I]f 'medievalism' [...] denotes
the whole range of postmedieval engagement with the Middle
Ages, then 'medieval studies' themselves must be considered
a facet of medievalism rather than the other way around."[51] Most
academic medievalists distinguish themselves from extra

academic lovers of medieval culture only by the degree to which they depersonalize their desire for the past, sublimate that desire into scientific and science-like practices, and share their activities with others.

Manifesto Two

The most exciting new forms of engagement with medievalia in the last three decades have originated from the confluence of reception studies, feminism, women's studies, and medievalism studies. They have managed to challenge the pastism of Medieval Studies, whose practitioners still prefer to see an insurmountable otherness in medieval culture. One of the most successful examples of a critical corrective to the alterity in traditional Medieval Studies is Juanita Feros Ruys and Louise D'Arcens's essay collection, *"Maistresse of My Wit": Medieval Women, Modern Scholars* (2004). Openly playful, the contributors to this volume combine presentist empathy, memory, subjectivity, resonance, affection, desire, passion, speculation, fiction, imagination, and positionality with the existing body of modern scholarship and its practices. In their experimental combination of enthusiastic presentism and scholarship, they equal the collaborative spirit of Guédelon-builder Michel Guyot and his academic advisory board. I am convinced that the best medieval scholarship of the future will be similarly conscious of its own investigating subjects' role in the long history of the reception of the medieval artefact or practice under investigation.

Manifesto Three

Pastist medieval studies is based on a predigital and hierarchical culture of knowledge production and reception.

Within this culture, access to information (manuscripts, editions, and similar) was controlled and granted by gate-keeping specialists, institutions of higher learning, research libraries, and publishers. Scholarship was written for and distributed among specialists, and making one's work inaccessible (linguistically, economically, hermeneutically) to larger audiences was almost a precondition to success among one's colleagues. How well has that worked for us? Of around 1.5 million peer-reviewed articles published annually, most are completely ignored. In the humanities, 82 per cent of such articles are never cited; in the social and natural sciences fewer than one-third of such articles are cited, and only about one-fifth of these cited papers were actually read. Overall, an average paper in a peer-reviewed journal is read completely at most by no more than ten people; and one shudders to think of the distribution statistics of essays published in essay collections or *Festschriften*.[52] Given the (partly self-sought) splendid isolation of medieval studies from the public, should we be surprised when two hundred years of academic scholarship—mostly disseminated amongst ourselves, providing detailed evidence that the *ius primae noctis* or Right of the Lord's First Night was never actually practised, but was a rhetorical and fictional device invented by the medieval and early modern nobility—can be obliterated by one single 177-minute *Braveheart*-rending blockbuster featuring Mad Max Mel Gibson?

Manifesto Four

In recent years, some of the most influential impulses for smart and public-facing engagement with medieval culture have come from para- and extra-academic publications and genres. The BABEL-affiliated blog, *In the Medieval Middle* (http://www.inthemedievalmiddle.com), for example, has enticed thousands of colleagues to see their medievalist practices no longer in isolation, but in intimate connection with their personal paths as well as current political and general academic debates. Free from the only sometimes enabling obstacles of academic writing, the blog has also empowered scholars to view the medievalist practices of our academic forebears in these forebears' own personal, political, and academic contexts, and to recognize these forebears' own unacknowledged indebtedness to layer upon layer of reception histories of original medieval artefacts.

Other blogs, like Paul Sturtevant's *The Public Medievalist* (http://www.publicmedievalist.com), fulfil the ethical obligation academic medievalists have to put their specialist education to serve the very public that makes that education possible. On May 12, 2016, Sturtevant published an extensive blog in which he demonstrated how the military flail, which has been featured in novels, movies, and even museums as a medieval weapon, is really part of the postmedieval invention of what the Middle Ages were like.[53] Perhaps in part because the cultural phenomenon of medievalism includes those fascinated by the history of war, battles, and certain kinds of masculinity (a sometimes darker side of medievalism we need to face), the post reached and critically engaged more readers than dozens of scholarly limited-access publications on the topic. The same is true for the increasing number of public medievalists who engage in public debates in established news media and, thus, demonstrate the contribution academic scholars can make to the cultural work in which all citizens can potentially participate. Too many academic rituals, specifically written and unwritten guidelines for hiring, tenure, promotions, and awards, still explicitly exclude work in the public humanities as enhancing one's academic record. We need to change that. Writing for broader publics and engaging with local and regional communities is a valuable competency, a specific form of professional communication substantially different from that which we practise when addressing other specialists. Just like classroom teaching, it is research that reaches out, gives back, and transforms. It is something we should cherish, not demean as somehow ignoble.

Manifesto Five

In *Medievalism: A Critical History*, David Matthews has rightly called medievalism an "undiscipline" (178) which (like Cultural Studies) explodes existing canons, retrieves excluded voices, and remains in a state of productive uncertainty about its disciplinary boundaries. I would add that, even as such an "undiscipline," it has value in itself and not merely, as many professional medievalists still prefer to see it, a necessary boarding drug leading to reading and researching "real" medieval texts and artefacts. Medievalism is neither a "parasite" that inhabits and harms its host, the harmless academic medievalist, nor a "children's disease" that the adult medievalist just needs to outgrow, as Benoît Grevin has claimed.[54] However, his assertion only obfuscates the adult medievalist's continued (but severely sublimated) emotional attachment to engaging with aspects of medieval culture. In fact, medievalism and medieval studies have a mutually beneficial relationship, and a thorough understanding of the broader cultural phenomenon of medievalism enhances academic medievalists' tool kits by increasing their theoretical sophistication, critical self-awareness, and social impact.

Manifesto Six

I realize I ask for nothing less than a foundational change in the way we conceptualize what it means to be a member of the academy. In many ways, the modern university has retained some of the characteristics of its medieval origins, the cathedral schools. It is a place that often attracts those who specifically seek it out to devote their lives to living in small cell-like spaces to conduct research and work there alone or together with small groups of colleagues and disciples. This exclusivist devotion to a *vita contemplativa* (often grandiloquently termed "the life of the mind") has often resulted in an intentional removal of scholarly engagement from the allegedly madding crowd, an existence that views itself above and beyond all breathing human passion. Protected by tenure, a high privilege granted so that members of the academy might research and express controversial views without fear of losing our positions, scholars are supposed to do work that is beneficial to the society that has afforded us this privileged space. However, these protective ivory tower walls have resulted in a situation where too many have conveniently forgotten to repay the high privilege by actively connecting our scholarship with the public. Such public scholarship is hard work and demands a more adventurous and entrepreneurial kind of academic than the one we have too often attracted and rewarded over the last 130 years. It is the kind of academic who intervenes in public discussions, stands up to racist and sexist trolls on blogs, twitter, and the mainstream media, advocates for open (and even "Robin Hood") access to scholarship, and creates an academy in which even younger scholars may safely experiment with hybrid genres of communication as part of their officially recognized professional responsibilities.

This kind of medievalist, aware and inclusive of the desires and emotions that attract us to engaging with the past, and unafraid of the inevitable occasional conflict that regular rendezvous with non-academic audiences may offer, also embraces the opportunity of being more than a traditional hyper-specialized medievalist. Revolutionary new paths of accessing, checking, and comparing information make it much less necessary for us to focus on only one historical period for one's scholarship, an artificial condition imposed by modernist science-like historicism in the second half of the nineteenth century. Reception studies, which contests the traditional retelling or replicating of medieval culture's self-understandings (Leopold von Ranke's "real" history, based only on original texts) by traditional medieval studies, supports readings that allow us to realize the psychic continuity of humanity across centuries and thus reveals the constructed nature of subjectivity over time. Within the overarching concept of medievalism, scholars may engage with medieval as well as postmedieval subjectivities not as a reductivist undertaking, but as an intellectually more complete, comparatist, and sophisticated endeavour. Unshackled by the dated separation of historical periodicities and the debatable division between the investigating subject and any given academic subject of investigation, I foresee a more truly co-disciplinary, inclusive, democratic, and humanistic engagement with what we call, for better or worse, the Middle Ages.

Notes

51 "Shared Interests of *SIM* and *MFN* (Vols. 22 and 23)," *Medieval Feminist Newsletter* 23 (1997): 33–35 at 33.

52 Asit Biswas and Julian Kirchherr, "Citations are not Enough," *The Impact Blog* (London School of Economics and Political Science), April 9, 2015, blogs.lse.ac.uk/impactofsocialsciences/2015/04/09/academic-promotion-scholars-popular-media/ (accessed May 31, 2016)).

53 "The Curious Weapon That Didn't Exist," at http://www.publicmedievalist.com/curious-case-weapon-didnt-exist/ (accessed July 11, 2016). Similarly valuable blogs include www.medievalists.net, modernmedieval.blogspot.de, and www.modernitesmedievales.org.

54 "De l'usage du médiévalisme (et des études sur le médiévalisme...) en Histoire médiéval," *Ménestrel*, March 25, 2015, http://www.menestrel.fr/spip.php?rubrique2133&lang= (accessed June 9, 2016).

Further Reading

The following moderately annotated list mentions titles beyond those already mentioned and/or cited in my text. The list is not meant to be comprehensive, and I selected these titles because they are representative of certain focus areas in medievalism studies, including research methodologies, historical periods, and geographical and cultural traditions.

Bishop, Chris. *Medievalist Comics and the American Century*. Jackson: University of Mississippi Press, 2016.
> A tour de force through medievalist comics, including *Prince Valiant*, *The Green Arrow*, *The Mighty Thor*, *Conan the Barbarian*, *Red Sonja*, *Beowulf*, *Dragon Slayer*, and *Northlanders*.

The Cambridge Companion to Medievalism. Edited by Louise D'Arcens. Cambridge: Cambridge University Press, 2016.
> Foundational for anyone who is venturing into medievalism studies.

Camille, Michael. *The Gargoyles of Notre Dame: Medievalism and the Monsters of Modernity*. Chicago: University of Chicago Press, 2008.
> Investigates the modern restoration of the medieval cathedral of Notre Dame de Paris and demonstrates how "our" Middle Ages are the projections of our own fantasies and

anxieties onto a medieval building and its architectural features.

Carpegnia di Falconieri, Tommaso. *Medioevo militante: La politica di oggi alle prese con barbari e crociati*. Turin: Einaudi, 2011.
   An important analysis of political and social medievalisms since the 1960s in entertainment, citizen tournaments, Catholicism, and Italy's Northern League.

Chandler, Alice. *A Dream of Order: The Medieval Ideal in 19th-Century English Literature*. Lincoln: University of Nebraska Press, 1970.
   A foundational study of medievalism discussing the works of Walter Scott, William Cobbett, the Lake Poets, Thomas Carlyle, Benjamin Disraeli, John Ruskin, William Morris, and Henry Adams.

Cramer, Michael A. *Medieval Fantasy as Performance: The Society of Creative Anachronism and the Current Middle Ages*. Lanham: Scarecrow, 2010.
   The best study of recreational medievalism, written by a practitioner and critic.

D'Arcens, Louise. *Comic Medievalism: Laughing at the Middle Ages*. Cambridge: Brewer, 2014.
   Examines what about medieval culture made postmedievals laugh, from Don Quixote, Victorian theatre, and the Monty Python films through the booming medievalist heritage industry.

Digital Gaming Re-imagines the Middle Ages. Edited by Daniel T. Kline. New York: Routledge, 2014.
   Investigates how digital gaming translates, adapts, and remediates medieval stories, themes, characters, and tropes in interactive electronic environments.

Early Modern Medievalisms: The Interplay Between Scholarly Reflection and Artistic Production. Edited by Sophie Van Romburgh, Wim van Anrooij, and Alicia C. Montoya. Leiden: Brill, 2010.

> Contains important contributions on medievalisms before the term and the concept of a clearly defined Middle Ages existed.

Emery, Elizabeth. *Romancing the Cathedral: Gothic Architecture in Fin-de-Siècle France.* Albany: State University of New York Press, 2001.

> Reveals the continued popularity of the medieval cathedral during one of the most anti-clerical periods of French history.

Fradenburg, Louise. "'So That We May Speak of Them': Enjoying the Middle Ages." *New Literary History* 28 (1997): 205–30.

> Central to understanding our desire for the past and scholars' sublimation of that desire into specific academic practices.

Ganim, John. *Medievalism and Orientalism*. New York: Palgrave Macmillan, 2005.

> Examining examples from anthropology, popular culture, international expositions, gothic architecture, antiquarianism, gender studies, politics, religion, language, and race, this study reveals the complexities of East–West relations and identity formation.

Goebel, Stefan. *The Great War and Medieval Memory: War Remembrance and Medievalism in Britain and Germany, 1914-1940*. Cambridge: Cambridge University Press, 2009.

> Excellent resource on public commemorations of medieval culture.

Groebner, Valentin. *Das Mittelalter hört nicht auf: Über historisches Erzählen*. Munich: Beck, 2008.
    A medieval historian's manifesto about how to reform his discipline. Recommends that historians recognize their own inevitable imbrication with popular as well as scientific receptions of the past, and reconnect *Mediävismus* (medievalism) and *Mediävistik* (medieval studies).

Harty, Kevin J. *The Reel Middle Ages: American, Western and Eastern European, Middle Eastern and Asian Films about Medieval Europe*. 2nd ed. Jefferson: McFarland, 2006.
    A meticulously researched encyclopaedia of almost a thousand cinematic representations of medieval culture worldwide.

Haydock, Nickolas. *Movie Medievalism: The Imaginary Middle Ages*. Jefferson: McFarland, 2008.
    A great introduction to the medievalisms in popular film, including *First Knight, A Knight's Tale, The Messenger: The Story of Joan of Arc, Kingdom of Heaven, King Arthur, Night Watch*, and *The Da Vinci Code*.

Kreutziger-Herr, Annette. "Imagining Medieval Music: A Short History." *Studies in Medievalism* 14 (2005): 81–109.
    An invaluable survey of the postmedieval reception of medieval music.

Lindfield, Peter N. *Georgian Gothic: Medievalist Architecture, Furniture, and Interiors 1730–1840*. Woodbridge: Boydell, 2016.
    Extends traditional discussions of Georgian Gothic to a large number of eighteenth-century fashions, including Palladianism, Rococo, Neoclassicism, and antiquarianism.

Medievalism: Key Critical Terms. Edited by Elizabeth Emery and Richard Utz. Cambridge: Brewer, 2014.

Concise essays on essential vocabulary for medieval-ism studies: archive, authenticity, authority, Christianity, co-disciplinarity, continuity, feast, genealogy, gesture, Gothic, heresy, humour, lingua, love, memory, middle, modernity, monument, myth, play, presentism, primitive, purity, reenactment, resonance, simulacrum, spectacle, transfer, trauma, troubadour.

Médiévalisme: Modernité du Moyen Âge. Edited by Vincent Ferré. Paris: L'Harmattan, 2010.
Centring on the twentieth century and popular culture, the essays in this volume investigate varieties of French medi-evalism.

Medievalisms in the Postcolonial World: The Idea of "the Middle Ages" Outside Europe. Edited by Kathleen Davis and Nadia Altschul. Baltimore: Johns Hopkins University Press, 2009.
Extends discussions of medievalism to examples from Latin America, India, Africa, and the US.

Montoya, Alicia. *Medievalist Enlightenment: From Charles Per-rault to Jean-Jacques Rousseau*. Cambridge: Brewer, 2013.
Argues, against established opinion, that eighteenth-century medievalisms were simply a form of nostalgic longing for a bygone era, but rather a distinct variety of modernity.

La Naissance de la médiévistique: Les historiens et leurs sources en Europe au Moyen Age (XIXe–début du XXe siècle). Edited by Isabelle Guyot-Bachy and Jean-Marie Moeglin. Paris: Droz, 2015.
Extends the history of academic medieval studies to examples from Belgium, Hungary, Italy, Luxembourg, Poland, the Maghreb, and other less well-known national-ist and regionalist medievalist tempers.

Neomedievalism in the Media: Essays on Film, Television, and Electronic Games. Edited by Carol L. Robinson and Pamela Clements. Lewiston: Mellen, 2012.

A rich source for case studies on medievalist film, animé, television shows, and digital games.

Queer Movie Medievalisms. Edited by Tison Pugh and Kathleen Coyne Kelly. New York: Routledge, 2009.

Essays investigating how gender and sexuality are constructed in cinematic representations of the Middle Ages.

Stahuljak, Zrinka. *Pornographic Archaeology: Medicine, Medievalism, and the Invention of the French Nation*. University Park: University of Pennsylvania Press, 2012.

Reveals the importance of nineteenth-century views of medieval sexuality for modern French identity.

Utz, Richard. "Speaking of Medievalism: An Interview with Leslie J. Workman." In *Medievalism in the Modern World: Essays in Honour of Leslie Workman*, edited by Richard Utz and Tom Shippey, pp. 433–49. Turnhout: Brepols, 1998.

Recounts the founding of Anglo-American medievalism studies within its founder's biographical context.

Warren, Michelle R. *Creole Medievalism: Colonial France and Joseph Bédier's Middle Ages*. Minneapolis: University of Minnesota Press, 2011.

A study of one of the most famous modern medievalist scholars, and how his identity as a Frenchman from the island of Réunion shaped his nationalist academic work.

Workman, Leslie J. "Medievalism and Romanticism." *Poetica* 39–40 (1994): 1–34.

The classic essay by the founder of the study of medievalism in the English-speaking world. Distinguishes between medievalism (the revival of medieval culture) and romanticism and Victorianism (the survival of medieval culture).

Young, Helen. *Fantasy and Science Fiction Medievalisms: From Isaac Asimov to* A Game of Thrones. Amherst: Cambria Press, 2015.
Complicates traditional understandings of medievalism as a defining feature of fantasy, and as the antithesis of science fiction.